# A Memoir

Written by: Sharon Marlow

Published by: Draft 2 Digital

*A blend of late-night confessional meets hard-earned wisdom*

*with a glass of red wine and blues playing in the background*

*Dedicated to all the guys who gave me so much material to work with along the way*

NEXT

**First edition. August 15, 2025.**



ISBN: 979-8232534615

Written by Sharon Marlow.

Enjoy

Sharon Marlow

# NEXT...

**PRELUDE**:

You spend your entire adult life searching for the perfect mate, among other things. In this case, the search is for *Mr. Right*, the one who will complete you, enhance your life, travel with you on your journey, support you, and love you as best as he can. I've been there, searching, more times than I care to think about, but I'll admit it: there have been three marriages and a few near-perfect boyfriends over the years. But I wasn't giving up quite yet.

Basic ground rules were usually in place: communication, compromise, respect, chemistry, and even *The Five Love Languages* and attachment styles were acknowledged. Yet, somewhere along the way, it all unraveled. Whether it was because one of us stopped trying or because they just weren't cut out to be a good partner, the end result was the same. You give your best, stay longer than you should, and then, eventually, you pull the plug.

Fast forward to 2022/23. I honestly thought I had found the *One*. Everything lined up nicely. All the boxes were checked and flaws were minor–not even close to being deal breakers. The 80/20 rule (80% good, 20% not so good) was in place and secure. Never been happier. It was *the best* relationship I had been in thus far, or so I thought. I was at peace and able to focus on all the other aspects of my life that were needing my attention.

But as the title of this book, *NEXT*, so aptly suggests, it ended.

His reasons were mostly vague, under the guise of "...too many challenges." What the hell were they? I may never really know. But to him they were challenges. That's what *he* decided. So, without our usual trademark, never fail, honest and loving discussions we pinky swore to always have, he threw me and *It* all away.

"Have a lovely evening" were his parting words!

But as the adage goes: If he was the *right* guy, he would have stayed.

So, this story is about what happened ***NEXT***.

Note: All or most of the names have been changed to protect the *not so innocent*.

# Chapter 1

It started with a flood. Not the big flood of Noah's era, but the flood of Daniel's Way–which still sounded rather biblical–and also my residence at the time.

The cause? Broken pipes on the 2nd floor of my apartment building, complete with surging waterfalls through ceiling tiles that shut down that floor, the lobby and the elevator for 2 weeks! Living on the 5th floor (technically the 6th if you count the parkade) was far from ideal. Every day felt like a small expedition just to get from my little suite in the sky down to the "mainland."

At first, the trek sounded daunting — a daily reminder that I was no longer the younger, fitter version of myself. In that moment, I felt old. But as my mindset shifted and determination set in, the angst, frustration, and constant muttering melted away. I even started to find a silver lining.

Then there was the question of survival — namely, how to haul food up the winding stairwell without wrecking my already fragile back. God forbid I missed a step and went tumbling to my doom!

The plan was to break up the process into manageable portions. I scheduled shopping days for each of the various food groups, and using a backpack, I precariously huffed and puffed up the daunting staircase as though I was in a Rocky 2 boot camp. To that end, I was successful in getting food back to my fridge, food in my belly, and muscles in my legs!! A direction that had its benefits.

Looking for ways to bring me joy and keep up my spirits, I was trying to focus on any positives that came my way.

One such event, which ended poorly but still had perks, was a trip to Mexico in February with my now ex-lover, Keith—the man I thought I would spend my life with. He was perfect. We were crazy in love. We conquered everything together. We communicated regularly. But, as alluded to earlier, and further expanded on below, it wasn't meant to be.

With that aside, we were staying at a lovely hotel at the Maya Riviera–top floor facing the beautiful ocean. Unfortunately, the elevators were located at the very end of the complex, *miles* away from our room in paradise. The stairwell, however, was right beside us, so for another week I scaled the stairs–usually half drunk on Margaritas—several times a day, and the glutes got even stronger. So all in all, I was now in pretty good shape.

The downside, after our return from the Mayan Sun, was that old *Don Juan was no longer the "one" as he* decided to break up with me the very next day.

In a daze and heartbroken (but with a great tan!) I struggled to make sense of it all. Where had it gone wrong? Attempts to plead my case for staying together failed as I rambled on the phone to him the next day. I tried to mask the pain but he had already made up his mind.

A few days later I sent a heartfelt email trying to defend our relationship and all the beauty it held but he was determined to be an idiot, not realizing what he had lost.

I was quite a mess for at least a week, staring at my walls, and barely moving, eating or breathing. Devouring everything I could find on the internet on how to get over a breakup and move on, I read inspirational quotes, made a list of all of Keith's flaws, and repeated them as daily mantras.

To add to the gloom, it was only two days before my birthday and we had planned to have a beautiful, romantic dinner. Instead, I faked my happiness at my family birthday party and quietly blew out my candles with tears spilling from my eyes.

The next week, I began to come around. Slowly. It felt forced. It felt icky. But I pulled up my big girl panties and started texting *all* my girlfriends. I booked myself solid with lunches, dinners, drinks for the next four days. As I spilled my sad story, they listened, they consoled, they spat on his mere existence and told me I was better off without him.

From that, I slowly started to mend.

The following week, I signed up on several dating sites. Was it a band-aid solution? Definitely. But I hoped it would inject a shot of dopamine to boost my spirits. "Let's see who else is out there." With my iPhone, my Apps and, of course, a glass of my best red in my opposite hand, I opened the gates.

No surprise, the pickin's were slim—very slim. Especially the over 60 crowd. Apparently it's a time/place where they go to die, or just get fat, wear old man glasses, stop combing their hair (if they had any left) and take selfies so you mostly see their double chins and their nose hairs trying to escape.

One guy, believe it or not, posted a picture of himself with oxygen tubes in his nostrils, recovering in a hospital bed. Sympathy vote? At least that one made me laugh hysterically, which was much needed.

As I swiped left, in groups of 50, there were maybe one or two that were worthy of a possible swipe to the right. It was disheartening to say the least. So I expanded my search criteria, but there was not much improvement. Again, there's something about that 60 mark. It's a black hole of lost souls. Men who have given up.

In between endless and frustrating searches on Tinder, Match and Bumble, I continued scheduling things to lift my spirits. I did some modeling for a fav store of mine called Lola's. Beautiful clothes. All overpriced but I was still occasionally tempted into the retail therapy trap, buying items I couldn't really afford.

On the bright side, it was a fun evening and I got to channel my inner Heidi Klum the best I could. I also found a new wine. "Butter Nut, Cab Sav." Rich, smooth, dangerous. Naturally, I went out and bought a couple of bottles the next day, which lasted all of three days. In my defense, I was still in heart break mode.

St. Patrick's Day provided another reason to get out with the gal pals, and we hit a restaurant to celebrate all that is green. My friend, Mel, who had her own personal dating battles, was more than happy to share/compare war stories as we both cried, figuratively, in our green beer. Nonetheless, it was part therapy and part checking out guys that *weren't* on dating sites. Sadly, things were not much better in real life.

As the third week of March began, I started to feel a shift back to my new/old self. I continued to fill my days with little things that brought me joy, or at least distracted me for a bit. But being unemployed, at the same time as being in heartbreak mode, was not a great combo. My distractions had to be staggered strategically throughout the day just to make it to bedtime. Sleep was my friend, my escape.

I started adding daily affirmation to my morning regime. I heard they helped for all recovery situations, so I incorporated them religiously, every day after breakfast.

Very ceremoniously, I would turn to the sunlight streaming in my kitchen window, throw my arms up to the sky as though I was praising a god, and announced my daily affirmations out loud.

Apparently, though, I was doing them wrong at first. I was supposed to recite them as though they had already happened. I *am* happy, beautiful, strong, employed, have the love of my life and my painful back issues have magically disappeared.

Initially, it felt strange, but as I continued on they became addictive and exhilarating. Sometimes I'd do them twice a day because it felt so good for the soul.

So what resulted from this renewed positivity? Well, first I joined a Facebook Group called "*WOW – Women of Windermere*." It's a local community group of ladies who provide support, information, nights out and everything else you can think of. It was enlightening. And will be referenced a few times in my story.

One day, I posted that I was unemployed and going through a breakup, which tugged at the heartstrings of one page follower. She had connections and offered me a complimentary facial/spa treatment at a new facility that had just opened in a neighbouring community. No charge. Free! Wow! How sweet.

I booked my spa escape for the facial later that week and it was completely divine. My skin felt like satin and I looked even younger than I apparently already do. When I told the esthetician my age, she actually blurted out, "Fuck!" and then apologized. She was shocked, and I was pleased that I could still get that reaction.

Meanwhile, back at the dating site ranch, I managed to lasso a couple of guys that I felt might be compatible.

The first guy, Ed, was someone I actually remembered seeing on a dating site a year earlier. Apparently he hadn't found the *One* either. He was handsome enough and he hadn't given up, even though he was passed the 60 mark.

His back story and his attributes checked out and we texted a few times online before we met. He thought I was *hot* and, apparently, as I later found out, was somewhat desperate to find a woman.

I will summarize our encounter as a four-hour-long discussion–or perhaps I should say confession—about our sex lives. Since I don't shy away from such topics, it was most entertaining, and I believe I supplied him with enough *material* to get him through the week.

That said, I did find him both appealing and intriguing. To say the least, it was a hot date and was stretched out over four separate venues, so we could keep the energy flowing.

A second date was scheduled in hopes of learning about the other side of Ed–if there even was one.

Meanwhile, I had another date the following night with a guy named Michael.

Total opposite of the Ed Conversation. We talked about everything except sex. But it was very interesting and he was now on the *keeper list*."

The deets on Mike? Hold my beer.

He was 57 years old (so he hadn't given up yet), spoke 3 languages beside English, was handsome, owned his own home in a prestigious neighborhood, had too many cars (so sold a few – *casual flex*), had secured his Masters in computer science, was an IT consultant, had skipped two grades in high school, worked out regularly, and loved clothes and shoes–as much as me.

To add to the whole package, he was very well-traveled and had lived in a few different places around the world. Originally from an exotic little island off the east coast of Africa, Michael was a self-proclaimed "beach bum" (I do *love* the ocean), enjoyed a glass or two of wine, was a gourmet chef, was romantic, loved music–especially when he was cooking (faint sigh), lived in the same area of the city as I did, and believed in the magic of dragonflies, which is another story for another time. He was also a Libra, if that holds any weight.

As the date continued, we discovered that we shared a lot of similar views, morals and attitudes on life. Since I was intrigued to learn more, another date was penciled in with the goal of getting into more *personal* stuff.

We gotta find the sizzle, people!

Feeling that my *dance card* was full enough, I placed my dating profiles in stealth mode so I wouldn't lure in anyone else. Two at a time was plenty.

As my affirmations and positive attitude continued, I went on to seek more adventures, or to put it mildly: things to bring me joy.

For example, flashing back to the old days, when I briefly partied with Alice Cooper's drummer, Whitey Glan. I often spill this story when my buds and I get chatting about celebrities we've met. Kind of like the Six Degrees of Kevin Bacon." Give it a Google if you're not familiar.

I was with my first, and now late husband, who was in an ancient band called "*Privilege*." Only Edmontonians of a certain age group will recognize the name.

Anyway, it was the 70s, and we went for dinner at a restaurant called Le Petite France. Whitey was with his girlfriend, Michele Finney. She wasn't well known (at least within my group of friends), but she had been on a TV show when I was a kid called "*Razzle Dazzle.*" She cohosted with another Canadian celebrity, Al Hamil, who was married to the late Suzanne Somers (who almost everyone knows).

I had been thinking about Michele and, out of curiosity, did a Google dive to see where she was now. I discovered her on Facebook, so I naturally checked out her profile and then took the leap to DM her.

Basically, I introduced myself and asked if she remembered me and my then husband, Corey (his nickname) and our dinner at La Petite France.

Very surprisingly, she replied within minutes! Yes! She remembered me and brought me up to speed on her life. Apparently, Whitey, whose real name was Pentti, had passed away about five years earlier and she was remarried to a famous guitarist and living in Ontario. Michele was and is an actress and did star in a few productions, so it was super cool to have a conversation with her.

She was very happy that I reached out and enjoyed reminiscing with me. We agreed that we should stay in touch now and then, if only via Facebook. The residual effects of our virtual chat left me in such a lovely mood and proud that I made the effort to add a little sparkle to my life by reconnecting with her.

The next day, March 28th, while out running some errands I stopped to grab a coffee at Starbucks in my neighbourhood. As I got out of my car, I noticed a woman sitting in an SUV, parked slightly off to the side.

Now, I never forget a face, although names escape me within seconds. I pondered for a few moments and concluded that she might be the gal who married a local celebrity DJ that I had dated shortly after my second divorce. So, I approached her and said, "Hello, sorry to bother you, but are married to John?"

Naturally, she gave me a, who-the-fuck-are-you-? look, but I quickly introduced myself and provided pertinent background to put her at ease. The penny finally dropped and we got into a very lengthy conversation about her husband.

I already knew that he suffers from Huntington's disease, and I had been very curious over the years as to how he was doing. She was kind and open, bringing me up to speed, and telling me all the things she was doing to bring awareness to the disease, including a Zoom meeting with Deena Henshaw, a prominent health spokesperson during the Covid outbreak era.

As the conversation continued to flow for about another 20 minutes—just long enough for my lower back to start yelling at me—she coincidentally received a phone call from her DJ hubby, so I got to say hello in a very short but sweet exchange, as he struggled with his words.

It was no surprise that he remembered me, as we did have quite the intense whirlwind romance.

So, once again, another chance encounter with someone from my past, who I had genuinely been wondering and worrying about, left me feeling better. I walked away relieved to know he was doing as well as could be expected and staying positive.

*(And short note to self and a pat on the back ... Yay! I'm writing again! Like a Phoenix, she has risen once more...)*

# Chapter 2

March had come to an end and I had survived my first breakup month. I had dusted off the remnants (and stench) of the *Keith era* and was on to the second date with Ed.

As expected, based on our previous encounter, we talked about sexual scenarios, desires and fantasies. This might turn some women off, but my interest in him and the chemistry between us was obvious, so it kept it exciting as opposed to weird or sleazy.

Our date, again, involved three venues. It was a very odd dating style to say the least: progressive dining meets wandering romance.

We started at one restaurant for lunch, which ended up being almost free as the meal was terrible and we had no choice but to complain. They comped most of our bill, so free lunch! Bonus.

From there, we strolled to the adjacent restaurant to have a glass of wine and chat some more. It was at this point that things started to heat up (hand on my leg and the overwhelming desire to kiss him). But the day was still young and we didn't want to rush things.

Not wanting to keep adding to our ongoing tab, we sauntered over to a local hardware store that shared a parking lot with the restaurant. In defense of the last venue choice, he did have a few things he wanted to look at and I'm always up for a stroll through "hardware." Romance has no terrestrial limits.

Meandering somewhere between garden hoses and paint supplies, I took the leap, grabbed his coat and pulled him in for a kiss. Good thing we were in a public place or who knows what might have happened? (Probably nothing, but the mind dared to wander).

Eventually, the hardware date concluded—I *did* have other things to do! We walked out to our cars, and again things heated up. This time the kiss wasn't so tame. Just two crazy *old* people making out in the parking lot. Nothing to see here, folks!

However, the kissing was compatible and the sparks confirmed it. On to planning date number three.

On the dating backstage, I kept getting very platonic-level texts from Michael. He wanted to let me know about the gas prices at Costco and that he was "now heading home."

*Riveting.*

If this guy was trying to woo me, he was going about it all wrong. Unbeknownst to him, he was losing ground quickly to *Fast Eddie*, and potentially eating our dust.

As mentioned earlier, Mike is great on paper. He's the kind of guy your friends–and therapist—would approve of to lock down. But trying to land that second date, which he did agree on, was still a flickering mirage in the dating desert.

Not even a flirtatious comment from this guy. Sure, I could have started that ball rolling—apparently, I'm an expert at flirting—but I was trying to give him the power of seduction. (insert yawn....) C'mon Mikey! I'm trying to write a story here! You've got the right ingredients, but there's no sizzle on the grill.

And to that end, Michael finally texted me back a few days later with an actual date request. Cue the fireworks!

Meanwhile, my connection with Ed was ramping up. Dare I say bonding (not bondage... well, maybe later) had begun? We had yet to consummate our relationship, but once that day came (pun intended), Mr. Mike would most likely get dropped. But it would be kind and gentle, with a possible Costco Gift Card to refuel his tank.

The text from Michael, after trying to line up our schedules, did say, "Definitely next Saturday."

But who knew? I could be practically married to Ed by then.

A girlfriend, who'd been keeping a running score card, predicted, "You'll be looking for wedding venues by next Saturday." If nothing else, we were keeping a sense of humour through all the chaos.

# Chapter 3

Aside from the dating world, I decided to apply for a job as a medical office assistant on the main floor clinic in the apartment building where I lived at the time. Talk about convenient! My only concern? My poor vehicle might start to rust (and dust) up in the underground parkade due to lack of use—much like me if I didn't get to spin *my* wheels soon.

There are pros and cons to everything. But that was a bridge I would cross when and if I got to it. With resumes also out to many other *perfect* places to work, I left it up to the universe to put me where I belonged. I had lined up for a face painting gig I thought I would try, but was still awaiting training.

While my work life was in limbo, my neighbour down the hall was preparing to go to a special clinic in Amsterdam in early April for unresolved PTSD treatment. I wanted to send her off with something thoughtful to promote her healing, so I purchased a beautiful journal and affirmation cards to help her on her journey. I left it at her door and then sent her a text that I had left a little gift for her.

She got back to me saying I was, "by far the kindest soul." She thought it was absolutely beautiful and very caring–she "truly loved it." I always know when I get the right gift or card, because I start to tear up myself. We empaths lead very emotional lives.

The next day started with good memories, and some sad ones, as I thought about my first husband and father to my children. It was April 4th, his birthday. A soul taken too early by cancer in the year

2000 at the young age of 45. It was one of those days where I felt the loss a bit harder.

So, my morning was spent delving into the spiritual world as I felt that it was calling. I looked for subtle signs that he was present while attempting to stir up my psychic side. *Perhaps* I did tap into something; a song started playing on my Spotify music track that was applicable. Several of lines stood out:

*I know I hurt you.*

*I hope you have found happiness.*

*I will be waiting for you."*

The last line was especially moving. Twenty-plus years have passed and still the sadness and emotions are there–always near the surface.

Feeling as though I had reached out as much as humanly possible into the ethereal mist, I pulled it together, jumped in the shower and headed out for some retail therapy. It was either that or stay home and dust and vacuum, which just felt criminal. Besides, it was an opportunity to rack up some steps for my health!

Never a day without sunshine—literally and figuratively. A tiny fragment of surprise happened while I sat in my car replying to text messages before heading into Edmonton's infamous Mall. A well-dressed and beautifully mature woman, outfitted in a stylish leather jacket, trendsetting glasses, tousled grey hair and a pop of bright lipstick, approached my car with a quizzical smile.

I rolled my window down to greet her and see what she wanted. Apparently, she was admiring my car (a 2015 Hyundai Elantra Sport). She was giving it the once over and wondered if she could take a picture of it. Weird, by okay. She pointed out her sweet ride a few cars over, a dark green Infiniti, and said it was time for a change. She liked the sportiness of my silver baby and wanted to get something like it. So, we exchanged a bit of car talk—*as women like to do*, and concluded that she needed to let her husband know what vehicle she would like next.

Just another day in a parking lot! I love spontaneous human interactions like this. So fun and unexpected.

The next day, in all its beauty and *more* sunshine, I dropped off my car for the seasonal tire switch and minimum maintenance. Painful, but necessary; I hate spending money on all things motorized. Plus; I was still unemployed and scrimping by on the last bit of my severance pay.

But as I digress for a moment, I still had to contend with a fractured *relationship* nearing its end.

I'd had a lengthy tête-à-tête with Ed the night before about *all things sexual.*" No surprise–we were in a loop. We dove into a lot of crazy and perverse areas and shared a few more ideas for our first *potential* encounter. I'll refrain from disclosing the details.

After the call ended, I started to process all that was discussed, and there were a few red flags, a few odd expectations, and a realization that this really wasn't the road I wanted to travel.

I freely admit that sexual encounters, either romantically intimate or just a wild and crazy ride, are in the top five on my relationship checklist. But it seemed that Ed could only focus on that subject. Ad nauseum.

I spent part of my sleepy time ritual that night, ruminating over points that had been made and rehearsing counterpoints in my head. His expectations were not my expectations, especially not on a daily basis. In the end, I decided I would revisit it in the next day or two and dissect our thoughts in unison. But I was spared the need to do that. The next day, Ed texted me, saying, "After sleeping on it I don't think I'm ready to have sex yet."

"At least we were on the same page there! I replied, "No worries, I don't think you are either."

It seemed that Ed was eager to talk about sex, but he was not ready (or able) to actually take the *plunge*. Thus, the endless fantasizing on his part.

I totally understand that when a guy reaches 60 and beyond, the *equipment* doesn't always rise to the occasion, even with the support of the Pfizer Empire. And I could tell he was very stressed about it as he had mentioned that he didn't want to disappoint me.

This is where I started to make the decision that, in the long run, this relationship was not going to work. Not just because of the sex but because I believed we wanted different things, generally, in life.

He liked fast food and avoided fancier restaurants. I love to dine out.

He worked crazy shifts so I could only see him on Saturday and Sunday afternoons —though he had planned to change this schedule.

I liked more romance and he lived mostly in his head where crazy shit was going down.

And when I suggested I cook a great meal for him (I *know* how to spice up a dish), he replied by saying he "may not like what I cook." Yikes!

Also, he didn't have any children, which may have been a factor when it came to family matters.

In the end, I listened to my gut and cut the ties, but I had yet to officially update him.

Onward, and maybe upward, to the elusive Michael, who at this point had only one foot into this whole dating thing. I could barely *buy* a second date, although he had *committed* to the *next* Saturday.

Or would Antoni (his profile "spelling") be the next one? I found this latest addition to the lineup on Tinder when he *pinged* as a mutual like/interest." We exchanged a few small-talk texts to get the ball rolling, but I was on the fence about him. His profile felt fake. My cultivated suspicions: he was very handsome, had high-quality photos (not the norm), said he was an engineer and had his masters. The Four Top Scammer Flags were flapping in the wind. He did agree to meet me the following week, but then—Poof—into the wind he dissipated, ghosting me without another response.

Not one to hang onto evaporated ghouls, I sent my *Dear John* text to Ed on Good Friday. Probably not so *good* for him, however. I kindly and gently let him know that after much consideration following our lengthy phone call the previous day, I felt it wouldn't work in the long term.

He wanted, or perhaps needed, a constant IV drip of sexual scenarios and fantasies that just weren't sustainable. Sure, I could entertain 50 Shades of indiscriminate colors, but not 24/7. Besides, there were so many red flags, even a Matador's bull would've collapsed from sheer exhaustion.

He seemed like he lived in his head where Porn Hub meets Larry Flint meets Charles Manson. Okay, maybe not the latter, but I wasn't going to slip into Stepford Wife stilettos unless it was a rare special occasion.

Although, part of me felt sad about his apparent performance issues, among his short comings, I didn't need a project.

With mild hesitation, I hit *Send* and waited for his reply.

A few moments later... Ding!

Ed: “Ok. Alright.”

I guess that’s all he could muster. ☹

# Chapter 4

Doing a complete switch-a-roo on the dating topic, I stumbled across an *intention* that was noted on a horoscope website I unintentionally follow (It's more like it follows me) that claimed I was in a psychic and empathic phase right then and would be connecting more with the spiritual world. It brought me back to that tearful day when I was trying to reunite with my late husband by grasping for symbolic signs from the beyond.

Of course, the mind can twist things to make you believe—like the song that was playing on Spotify during my mini séance. But I believe the pull to earthly dimensions from his children, sister and ex-partner were probably strong that day and perhaps that whole week.

Case in point, I was watching a movie the night prior called *Sam and Kate*. Very touching story to say the least, happy and sad all at once. During one of the scenes between Dustin Hoffman and Sissy Spacek, they got up to dance in her living room to the song *I Only Have Eyes for You*." I instantly teared up as that was our song back when we were dating and engaged. Because it's not a song you often hear, I wondered if it could be another sign?

To add to this memory, I woke up the following morning after a very intimate dream about my ex. It involved a very vivid encounter which, shall we say, ended well. Did he reach out to me again in my dream?

When I glanced over at my alarm clock, it said 8:34. That may be meaningless to most people, but I'm constantly seeing the number

34—on signs, clocks, license plates, receipts, anywhere there are numbers. From what I understand, it is a sign that the "angels are delivering a message or trying to get my attention." But again, perhaps it's all random. I chose to believe they were signs.

# Chapter 5

Back on the dating front, *fake* Antoni had definitely moved on, so no loss. However, Michael was confirmed for April 15, and the plan was to stir up some trouble with some intimate chit-chat.

He picked me up for our second date (likely straight from Costco fueling station) and off we went to an undisclosed location. He was trying to be mysterious.

We ended up at a lovely Italian restaurant, one that I had been to before–so good choice. He was a perfect gentleman, opening the car door for me, ordering a *whole* bottle of wine (impressive–and extra points) and stepped up to put my leftover pasta in the to-go box. Lovely gestures that I'm definitely not used to, but absolutely appreciated!

As the night was still young, we left and headed to another venue for more drinks and some cheeky banter. That's when things started to heat up with some playful and flirty exchanges. We had snagged a u-shaped booth, perfect for snuggling close, so as the night progressed, we shifted incrementally toward each other. Of course, innocently (or maybe not so innocently), I brought out my phone to show him some pix (that were relevant to a story I was telling, I swear), and I inched over even more. Leg/knee touching leg/knee, his hand resting lightly on my back, he now referred to me as "Honey." This was not the same studious Michael that presented himself earlier. As he leaned in, I could feel a spark catch between us.

Wine glasses now empty, the time had come to head out to his car. The moment we got in, he looked at me and said, "I've been waiting long enough," and leaned over and kissed me. Like *really* kissed me. It was good! But, like a rookie, I had already locked myself into my seat belt. So, we paused the moment and headed back to my apartment, hand in hand. With one of his hands, obviously, on the wheel.

Back at my building's entrance, we picked up where we left off (seat belt unbuckled this time), with some very passionate kissing. After quick contemplation, I said "I'd invite you up, but I don't think we're there yet. Are we?" And he replied "Yes, I'd like to come up." So, as anticipated to a certain degree, but not planned, we went upstairs. And then *it* happened. Oops!

The next few days, I worried that I might have given it away too soon. Did he still have a reason to chase me? Was he still interested? My anxious attachment style kicked in and I started overthinking everything. I think we may have floated the idea of another date, but I wasn't sure if it would transpire. Time would tell. He didn't come across as a player, so I thought we would be okay.

He did text me a few times, post *tumble,* so I thought I was still on his radar. The next short while I struggled to play it cool and not to reach out. However, I found an excuse to text him first by providing an update on the job interview I'd had. Did I get it... or not?

*I'd like to pause here to address how ridiculous and a bit insane it is that we, as women, feel we must play this game of the hunt. How many times have I read or heard, "Let them chase you – it's in their DNA." You mustn't look needy, clingy, desperate, weak, too interested... or human. Get busy with your life.*

Those words have become over-used clichés. The reason I'm dating is to add this piece to my already pretty good life. So, I wanted to focus on keeping the momentum going. I don't want to wait by the phone, hoping it will ring (or buzz or whatever the fuck it does now).

I wanted to be part of the hunt as well. (Still a cougar at heart).

Mid-April, and back to pursuing employment, I had an easy-going interview with an industrial company. Very informal and the job was pretty low-key. Main job was printing off labels for their cleaning products and then shipping them to the marketers. But a few days later they let me know that they offered the position to someone else, which was just as well. I would have been bored.

I had another job in the queue with an optometrist clinic. I had already done one assessment and then received another email the next day with questions geared to promote myself and why I am "just so awesome." I replied using my best skills, grammar and honesty to ensure a good fit, but as before, the position was offered to someone else. I guess we didn't see *eye to eye* after all.

I tried not to fall into a depression as all these rejections started to feel like... well, rejections. My daily affirmations were beginning to feel like broken promises. And who knew what kind of timetable they were on. It was like the breaking up emotions were still floating near the surface. And while I waited for another date with Michael, it almost felt like too much for one day.

Character Building 101 had turned into Character Building 1001.

If I were 40, I'd think, "Well, I have lots of years still ahead for great stuff to happen." But at 68, where the future is much, much shorter, I felt like I was running out of time. I was trying to trust the Universe to give me a break. Is anybody listening or have *they* all popped an Ativan and gone to sleep?

I knew I should be grateful for all I have....

But I was still muttering F-bombs in frustration.

As I struggled, specifically with relationships, I was still of the mindset that I must find a love that will take me to the day I depart to the Pearly Gates. I am a hopeless romantic. Always have been.

Despite all my failed relationships and marriages, I still loved to love. No matter how many great friends and loving family members, and, of course, my kids, my heart still desired romantic love.

I wanted to look after someone and feel needed, and to also have someone who felt the same way back. I loved sexy encounters, fun and silly things, little secrets kept between two lovers, hugs, kisses, touch, laughter–lots of laughter—cooking together, sharing vacations, memories, star gazing, moon watching, holding hands, whispering, massages, foot rubs, great conversations, great meals and traveling to new destinations.

(And yes, Miley Cyrus, I *can* buy myself flowers–but seriously girl, only for a couple of weeks!)

April 22–I hoped I'd be seeing Michael again. I let him know I didn't snag the job I wanted and hinted that I required some cheering up. I coyly asked if he had any suggestions (wink), but he didn't surface until the next morning. And that was by text! Pfft! He said he was at his cousin's watching the hockey game, but I'm sure at some point he glanced at his phone and registered my existence. Still, that's no excuse not to take the 20 seconds to let me know he was engaged in some heavy male bonding.

His sparse reply was, "Yes, we definitely have to make plans to cheer you up," but then nothing was offered. So, with nothing to lose, I stepped up and said, "What about tonight if you're free?"

Crickets.

Two hours passed. So jumping in with both feet, I offered a Plan B. "How about dinner – my place? I'll make gourmet," then added, "I'll need to step out to grab the special ingredients," hoping to prompt some urgency for his response. The manipulation worked and he replied very quickly, only to say he had a plumber coming over to fix his pipes (or whatever) and he wouldn't be able to meet up. A follow-up, "Rain check, baby, ttyl," was his best effort and concluded the convo. My best response effort: "The offer stands for tomorrow as well."

Meanwhile, I already started to cut the ties in my heart and head and take away two lessons from this last dating disaster.

Lesson #1: DON'T SLEEP WITH A GUY ON THE SECOND DATE!!

Lesson #2: Value yourself more than the guy.

Surprisingly, it felt liberating. I felt better and stronger. There was power in taking the high road and releasing wasted hope.

However, his ignoring me and aloofness aside, he would have been a great catch!

Damn!

# Chapter 6

## THE AWAKENING

April 23 – not sure if it was too early to claim "the awakening" but I felt like something had shifted. A new learned behaviour or reflex that I didn't have before. Something that was decades in the making, building, morphing, growing, changing and any other synonyms we can use for movement; movement of the soul to be more precise.

I had been thinking about how much I've been through in my life. Basically, since birth. Born and *rejected*, (although I know it wasn't quite like that), I was adopted. Like many others, I grew up in a somewhat dysfunctional family. Not horrid but bad enough at times. Bullied and abused in many forms by family, spouses, and even coworkers. Sexual abuse, emotional abuse, verbal abuse and a bit of physical abuse–enough to wear my self-esteem and self-worth down to a nub.

When I was 30 years old, I wrote a list titled: *30 Reasons Why I Hate Myself.*" I may even still have it tucked away in some dusty notebook and hidden in a shoebox. It had been a tough go but I survived, and around my $40^{th}$ birthday I went to see a shrink to untangle the mess. Oddly, but successfully, I had one of those *Aha!* moments during Eye Movement Desensitization and Reprocessing therapy (EMDR) that somehow cleared the demons and repressed memories from my mind.

I remember thinking the whole time how bogus this treatment felt. Like, seriously, moving my eyes back and forth? Pffft! Nonetheless,

I broke through the brick walls and made the biggest realization of my life. It wasn't *me*! It was *them*! I had been mistreated by men pretty much my whole life. It was astonishing that I even wanted to be on the same planet as a man.

And from that point on, I swore I would never be disrespected again. (That's not to say I didn't let a few tiny ones slip by).

Looking back at my life in general... Three marriages and three divorces. Then there was the terrible year I turned 30, when within a six-month period, my dog died, I got a divorce, my daughter failed a grade, my mom underwent a mastectomy for breast cancer and while she was in the hospital recovering, my dad died on our front doorstep from a heart attack. He had been heading to the hospital to visit my mom and was found the next morning by the paperboy.

During this time, I had also moved to Calgary, with my late husband, but with the divorce in the middle of it all, I returned to Edmonton to start over. Driving away in an old Fiat, my two small children in the back seat, and uncertainty riding shotgun, I had to find a job, a place to live, a school and daycare, along with the strength to survive.

That year I experienced numerous panic attacks, but by the grace of an exceptional doctor, who literally held my hand for 45 minutes while he taught me how to breathe through them, I conquered it all.

While life isn't always wonderful and cheery for very long (cue the rollercoaster cliché), I endured three failed marriages and the very sad, and too early, death of my first husband and father to my children. It was tough on all of us. My son dove into great depths of despair and grief, and I did my best to keep him afloat. My daughter was also grieving with the same intensity but she handled life a little better, generally, and had extended family to lean on as well.

On top of all of that, my work history almost became another story in itself. With repeated layoffs from 2014 onward—six to be exact—I was now suffering from PTSD every time a boss called me into their office just to chat. The last layoff occurred in May 2024 at a time when I should be retiring, not looking for another job.

Just for fun, let's sprinkle in a total of 20 residential moves in my lifetime–all due to various life changes.

Put all that shit in a bag and I think I've done well to not end up in some loonie bin. (Is that politically correct to say?).

So, that brings me, not only to writing this book, but to that awakening I mentioned. I finally had a clearer view of the path in front of me, and a better sense of myself and my worth and my value.

As noted previously, the daily affirmations had been a great help. They helped me reset my compass every day, and reminded me of my blessings and my gratitude. That is where I found this new clarity. Something else, whether better or worse, will come along. And it too will be temporary. And I will thrive or survive.

It also made it easier to date and reject the ones that would not measure up for the long term. And to accept the ones who have rejected *me*. But as I continue to apply the 80/20 rule for pretty much everything in life, I'm optimistic that I will find a romantic partner, someone to enjoy life with.

With that in mind, I lived each and every day to the fullest, doing as I pleased, slept when I ran out of energy, ate cereal for dinner and enjoyed the blessings of pretend retirement.

Meanwhile, back on the *love trail,* I received a text on a quiet Wednesday afternoon just as dusk was settling on the horizon.

"Ding."

I grabbed my phone nonchalantly and to my surprise... a text from my past lover, Keith. The one with "too many challenges."

My immediate reaction: WTF!?

I stared at the preview on the screen for a few minutes before fully opening the message.

*What could he be saying?*

*Do I want to know?*

*Is he crawling back to me on hands and knees?*

I felt irked. Pissed off.

*Why are you reaching out to me, you piece of shit?*

I tried to resist, but my curiosity got the better of me. After about 15 or 20 minutes I finally opened the full text bubble and read it. And this is how it went:

*Keith: "Just wondering how you're doing these days, my dear? Even though we're not together I often think about you, and hope that you're doing well.... (happy face inserted)."*

A whole 16 hours went by before I decided to reply. If I could make him squirm, this would be the time.

*ME: "Hey, yes, of course it's natural to think of past relationships. I'm doing very well. Staying busy, focusing on me and in a great place emotionally and spiritually... exactly where I need to be. Thanks for asking. I trust you're doing well. Enjoy your summer." (No emoji inserted)*

No response. I mean I was (*kinda*) expecting a short wrap rebuttal, like "Ok, that's great to hear. I'm doing well too."

Were my expectations so out of whack that I actually expected responses to questions or minor statements? Case in point, my last and final message to Michael to say, "I don't appreciate being disregarded and it wouldn't work out," never received a response either. I wasn't looking for fireworks and shooting stars. Just a speck of class and accountability.

But nope. Crickets, crickets and more crickets! *Locusts*! That will be my new term.

Of course, I had to tell my buddy, Mel, about this little encounter to get (and appreciate) her feedback. She felt the same way as I did. Why the hell is he reaching out? And why now?

When I mentioned to my friend he hadn't responded, she burst out laughing. "Girl, you just shut him down. He wasn't expecting that response. He was hoping to hear you were miserable."

And, of course, I knew that when I composed my reply. Not to say my words weren't true. I was feeling good, hopeful, content, but it's not what he wanted (or needed) to hear—or shall I say read?

Needless to say, he had reopened a can of hurt and residual anger, and I actually thought about what it would be like *if* I were to go back to him. Part of me was disgusted, still pissed and annoyed. But a very small part of me, like five percent entertained the thought briefly, bouncing scenarios around in my brain like emotional ping-pong.

In the end, I knew that I needed and deserved better than what he could offer me.

Time and distance had made my mind and soul see clearer. His faults became more obvious and I knew he wasn't the man for me.

Too routine

Too cautious

Too restricted and reserved

Too frugal – OMG! Total understatement!

And, let's be honest, too old in his thinking. He liked to hang out with seniors only (and pickle-ballers). I liked to hang with everyone!

# Chapter 7

May 15$^{th}$ started off slow. The kind of day you contemplate the alternatives to *life*." I moved like a sloth, entertained the need for a nap, and slogged through my exercises. Didn't do my daily affirmations. Decided no one was listening anyway. You know. That. Kind. Of. Day.

Not to waste an entire day wallowing, I headed out to meet a friend around 5:30 who had been one of my top fan art buyers. She had been eyeing one of my abstracts and decided to add it to her "Marlow Collection."

We planned to meet at Starbucks (my "go-to" coffee hub, which will be repeated throughout this story). However, when I arrived, she was wandering around the parking lot, a bit distracted, phone in hand. As suspected, she was sending me a text messages. The plan changed, and with a gift card in her hand, we navigated to another restaurant on the same lot. Coffee is good, but food and wine are better!

Oddly enough, this was where Keith and I had our first date on the second go round. We had dated for a few weeks about a year earlier, but he broke it off saying, "We are in different stages of our lives." But I had liked him enough to give it do-over... Second time's a charm, right? Not.

Anyway, my friend and I had a lovely early evening with a drink and some appies, and for about 15 minutes the conversation digressed to Keith. No surprise, since they were good friends, and that's how I met her. Lovely lady. She liked to golf, as I, and loved my art. Good combo and overlap.

After we had exhausted most topics of conversation and sealed the art deal, we bid our adieus. Thankfully, this small encounter helped to lift my mood and I was glad I got out of the house and reconnected with life and another human.

With a quick stop to the bank and art money deposited, I returned home. But with the lingering taste of a good wine still on my lips, I took a slight detour to the liquor store, dangerously located on the main level of my apartment. Another glass seemed appropriate to celebrate.

Cue my friendly, social-butterfly persona. I struck up a casual chat with the store attendant, who happened to live in my building. We knew each other fairly well — our paths often crossing in the elevator or, naturally, right there at the store. Without fail, he'd ask if I was "employed yet," since we had an ongoing "connection" on that particular subject.

"How are you doing? Did you find work yet?" he asked. Then he added, "So, what do you do all day?"

With a pouty sigh, I responded, "Nothing."

But then I opened up (fueled by the one glass of wine I imbibed earlier) and let him know that I was an artist and I was working on some new abstracts. I presented my Instagram account for reference, but he was already connecting to it via his phone–because he was younger and tech savvy...

I pulled up an awesome pic of a wine bottle and grapes and said, "This would look perfect in your store. Maybe you could help me sell it."

One thing led to another (as it always does) and suddenly I'm divulging my life story (again).

"So do your kids live with you"? he asked.

"No," I said, "they're all grown and have kids of their own."

"Oh, so do you live alone?", he continued to ask.

"I do." But as the words spilled from my mouth, I hit the verbal brakes and said, "But I'm not telling you which suite, as I don't want you knocking on my door."

His reply was, "Well, I live in suite 400, if you want to know." Apparently, he lives alone too!

Yikes.

*Now what can of worms did I open?!*

He followed up with, "If you get bored, you can always come down here and chat with me."

Now this is all wonderful on the surface, but I didn't want to invite unwelcome company. If he was handsome and closer to my age, this story might have a different spin. But he was only about 30ish, and not my type. Kind of nerdy, shy and unsure of himself (or maybe it was something else... I don't know). On the bright side, he did give me a 10% discount.

Moving forward, I had to be more careful! And watch my words... "Yup, I'm single and live alone... Come kill me."

I made a mental note to utilize the peephole in my door for a while after that.

Nonetheless, as my night progressed and I was back safely in my suite (alone), I was now bombarded with replies to a Facebook post I submitted earlier in the *WOW – Women of Windermere* group." As noted previously, it's an awesome group of ladies who get together for brunches and nights out, who are looking for references, hairstylists, pet sitters, handymen, etc. You name it, we're asking! So, I had posted: "Looking for ladies who golf," and boy did I get a response! Suddenly I had to coordinate golf outings with about 25 ladies for the daytime, evening and weekends. Who knew it would be this easy? Or this difficult to coordinate?

During this time, I also created a group called "Singles Mingles" to round up and coordinate with all the single ladies in our expansive community who were also on the hunt for quality men. Not surprisingly, the numbers grew in this group as well.

Finally, around 10:00, I put my phone down, poured myself a glass of (discounted) wine, wrote this submission into my book and planned to revisit scheduling golf games the next day.

With my social calendar possibly filled for the foreseeable future, my thoughts drifted back to the dating scene.

While I got ready for bed, a little gem I deemed worthy of honourable mention in the "you-can't-make-this-stuff-up" category, popped into my head.

On one of my dating profiles, I politely asked that if anyone posted a picture of themselves in sunglasses, to please have a second picture so I can, "...appreciate all of your facial features at the same time." I guess this was a real trigger for old Bill. I quote (spelling errors and all):

*Bill: "I'm not changing who I am for anyone if I want to where my sunglasses. I'm not asking anyone on here to change who they are or what they do. If it doesn't fit, it doesn't fit."*

Deep breath, Bill. Don't be fogging up those specs.

*Me: "Yup, Bill. You just keep being you. I'd hate to see your whole personality change just by taking off your sunglasses. Lol."*

Honestly, what's with that simple request that it triggers men into having full identity crises? I'm not asking for a blood sample, buddy. Just a face, preferably with eyes and teeth.

These are the nightmares of dating sites: But wait... There's more! Like six more. If you want to talk about the horrors, sign up on any of the popular "match-up" sites. They all reside on Elm Street. They're all scary.

Over of the course of about 10 days, I had been (very briefly) chatting with a total of six somewhat handsome men. Oddly and mysteriously, mid-convo they disappeared. Like POOF!" Gone. No retrieving. No search. Just vanished like a black sock in a dryer.

In hopes of a reasonable explanation, I contacted the dating site twice about this matter only to receive a very generic response noting they probably deleted their account or removed the match.

Okay, so I can see maybe one or two but this happened six times in a row, right around the 3rd text exchange. Their parting words (before getting sucked into the abyss) were along the lines of, "You have a great profile, I'd like to know more about you." To me (unless I'm just crazy), that would indicate they *are* interested, not about to pull the plug!

Never did hear back from the site on my second request (I guess they're *ghosting* me too), but I still requested a cancellation of my account and a refund! And yeah, I know, buyer beware. No surprise. Crickets.

But when the fake profiles start to out-number the real ones, it's time to move on. Money lost. Lesson learned.

The formula (aka, the *lesson*):

FAKE: The guy is handsome; photo quality is polished; he's an engineer, most likely a widow and he's *not* holding a fish.

REAL: The guy is border line hideous, scary, possibly cheating; photo quality is blurry or at a really bad angle, catching only the back of his head or his dog; or he's a speck in the horizon... next to a mountain... holding a fish. And like good old Bill from above, wearing sunglasses.

In hindsight, I think I should have taken my chances with the odd guy at the liquor store. At least he doesn't disappear. But then again... Eww.

# Chapter 8

On the financial side, I was still *surviving* without a paycheque.

Job hunting had shifted back to the top of the priority list, and with that came another interview. This time with a home builder. I was excited! I do love all things HGTV and home-related so my designer fingers were crossed! It was scheduled for a few days ahead, and I really, really hoped this would be my *forever job*.

To that end, I had come to the conclusion that I will never retire. The last six months, my incomeless, forced retirement, made me realize that I could never be a woman of leisure. I would aspire to being the next Betty White, working until the wheels fell off. Meanwhile, I had all this glorious free time to myself but no money to do anything.

If you can only stare at walls, go for a walk, buy bread and milk and count your quarters to buy a Starbucks coffee, then you might as well commit a crime and go to jail. The kind that Martha Stewart committed, not the Charles Manson kind.

Of course, I had to find a job I loved (if that was possible), and then it would be smooth sailing (but only on windless days, of course). And as we know, life is never going to give you windless days.

May 25th, another day on the calendar.

Still unemployed and staying hopeful. But another interesting day, nonetheless.

I went for my somewhat regular walk around the local pond to get some exercise and burn off the 5 tablespoons of ice cream I inhaled. (I know, I'm bad). I tried to unfriend food, or at least the bad food, as much as possible, in order to shed some belly blob. However, it seemed the less I ate the bigger it got.

It was time to jump on the fasting trend bandwagon, if only in baby spoon steps. Thirteen hours fasting and an 11-hour eating window, as long as that window didn't include a drive through. I knew that wasn't exactly how it worked, but I figured if I could stop eating after my evening meal, I could tough it out until breakfast the next morning, which was usually around 9:00. It was a start.

My goal for the pond walk was to breathe in some fresh air, *and* become miraculously skinny. The forest fires, at that time, had fizzled out and it was once again safe to inhale.

As usual, there were a few regulars – dog walkers, kids with no direction, and solo strollers, like me. Most offered a friendly, polite smile as we passed each other in opposite directions. But one particular dog-walker chirped up and said, "Lovely night for a walk," and I couldn't resist responding in full confessional mode.

"Yes, it is. Plus, I'm trying to wear off the ice cream I just ate."

Because why not divulge my dietary sins to a complete stranger?

And from there, the conversation took on a life of its own. She had laughed with agreement and shared she just started intermittent fasting too. I confessed that I just started about 15 minutes ago. (Again, my comedic edge) and the bonding ensued with more laughter.

At this point, I realized that we were on this walk together for the full loop. The conversation flowed like wine at girls' night, and we covered a lot of ground, both verbally and physically as we compared notes.

She was currently working from home but was usually lodged up in a town called Kitimat. Not many people probably know about that NW town in the province of BC, but I've been there (kind of against my will) and knew it well.

"Did a lot of fishing there with my ex-ex" I said.

So naturally she asked, "How many exes have you had?"

This led to a full-blown discussion about being single and dating sites and how impossibly hard it is to meet quality men. She revealed she dated a guy about 15 years younger than her, and I responded (with absolutely no shame) that "My younger guy was 20 years my junior." Definitely good for a quick laugh and a lusty confession on how great the sex was. Yup, you can't beat those young studs. Well, you can, but...

As the conversation progressed, she said she was doing stand-up comedy. How hilarious is that?! Can you imagine? *Two comedians walk into a bar....* (or around a pond, in this case)?

I let her know that my sense of humour was one of my greatest strengths (hence my self-proclaimed title: The Comedian") and one of my finer qualities listed on my dating profiles.

"It's important to find a guy with a great sense of humour as well," I noted. Otherwise, it's just a lot of awkward silences and explaining your jokes all the time.

Beyond our combined wit, a few other commonalities were exposed. We were both slightly OCD, single, living alone, loved the same movies (yep, we even got onto that topic) and gushed over Richard Gere from Pretty Woman. It's truly amazing the topics that women can cover in a short 30-minute period – comedy, fasting, exes, great sex, and rom-com heartthrobs. All the basics.

As our pond trek came to a close, I asked her where she lived.

"I live in the grey and blue apartments just up there," she said, pointing in their general direction.

"Well holy crap, so do I!"

And as we verbally pinged on our exact location, we discovered we lived on the same floor just a few doors apart! Crazy or what? It was then I engaged my memory bank and it all came flooding back. I *had* seen her (and her dog) in the elevator a few times, but hadn't really locked it into my brain, even though we had spoken. She started to remember me as well and we had another good laugh.

We exchanged phone numbers and I said, "Give me a text next time you're out walking your dog." (It's noteworthy to say at this point that she walked her dog *every day*.). Doggies do gotta pee.

Once off the elevator, we turned towards our respective apartments and said, "See ya later."

If only it was that easy to meet a nice guy!

# Chapter 9

June 5, 2023 – Life had been a bit of a flat-liner. Still looking for a job, still waiting to hear back from prospective employers. All in the works but nothing finalized. Tried for a job at the medical clinic in the building where I lived. Ride the elevator to work and, "I'm Here!" Car would probably rust up from lack of use if I got this job but obviously the big perk would be not having to drive, no white-knuckle commutes in the wintertime and never having to pack a lunch. Lunch would be waiting for me in my penthouse every day! (Yes, I know... penthouse sounds fancier than it was, but, hey, top floor, with 20' high ceilings qualified). Plus, I'd save a fortune on gas.

The other job – perfect for my passions, ideals, creativity and utilizing my civilian clothes (as opposed to scrubs), at a home builders paradise – HGTV here we come! Downside, it was downtown.

*Dowwwwwnnn towwwwnnnn. Argh! Not the route I wanted to travel.*

Forty-minute drive there and one hour crawl back. Insert grimace! (And back pain).

Practically my entire adult working life had been downtown, but I hadn't always lived this far away from City Central! Would it be heart over head, if there was a tie? One full time, one part time. In the end, if a choice needed to be made, I would follow my passion. Life's too short. Then again, the drive would be long.... I shut down the thought and decided to cross that bridge (or just the parking lot) when the time came.

In the end the decision was made for me. The dream job with the home builder fell through as they decided to put it on hold. The medical office position in my building never got back to me, even after I presented my bubbling personality during the meet and greet with the doctor. I did follow-up with a "Hello?" email, but it had already flat-lined. So again, eff that.

Keep trying and applying. NEXT! NEXT! NEXT!

# Chapter 10

Meanwhile, I was still losing to the dating sites. *(Along with millions of other hopeful single women).*

I heard, via somewhat reliable sources, that Tinder (and probably many others) reported that 1 in every 10 profiles is fake? Do the math, dear reader! That's insane. Like what's the point. Why am I bothering?

I decided to let my subscriptions expire. Come September, the financial ties would be cut and I would *never* go near a dating site again. I would submit to a life of nun-hood before venturing down that black hole of ugliness.

With a few months grace on the dating site, I was still classified as "active", and with that another ping made its way through. In true Pavlovian form, I answered a new prompt hoping that I had finally stumbled across a *real* guy this time. He sounded normal. His name was Don. Good grammar. Reasonably well-balanced.

I asked for his phone number right away, explaining that the system kept removing profiles mid-sentence. Six in a row! Gone. Poof. Like they had vanished into some weird dating Bermuda Triangle.

So, he kindly gave me his phone number. Then as the days passed and the texts volleyed back and forth, I noticed something odd. The grammar got weird. Overly formal and the syntax got out of whack.

I received texts like, *"I would NEVER try and actually find you & presumably, if we were going to meet, you were to give me suitable enough instructions that I would actually be able to find you",* later followed by *"I will come back when I have more moments."*

Seriously, who talks like this post the Shakespearian era?

Anyway, you get the gist of it.

So, because I'm unemployed (I did say that before... right?) I had lots of time to do some sleuthing. I did a reverse search on his phone number and lo and behold the golden gates of the Internet opened (insert light beam here).

Within that beam, I discovered his last name, unearthed him on LinkedIn and Facebook, extracted where he works and, believe it or not, zoomed in on his home on Google Maps. I was in full stalker mode. This, my friends, is how generous the Internet can be, even when doing a basic search.

On the surface, it seemed like the code was cracked and Don was, in fact, real. But I still felt something was off. Possibly due to the grammar from *Hamlet*.

He had two LinkedIn accounts. One with his picture, lots of details on his job history and 500+ connections. All there for the taking. The other LinkedIn profile had only his name, no picture and no connections or posts. This also applied to his Facebook page. It appeared that Don had opened his Facebook account that January, had no posts, three friends – two of which were of Russian decent, and the one photo of himself which he also used on his Tinder account.

His last text to me was that he had "come down with a cold, very sore throat and wasn't going anywhere." I was thinking, classic rebuttal. Nonetheless, I decided to give him a call at his office. You know, see how he was doing and if the chicken soup he claimed to be curing himself with, had worked.

The secretary picked up the phone–polite and professional–and informed me that Don was in a meeting at the moment (*in* the office – not on Zoom) and that I could reach him later on his cell. To his credit, it was the same number he gave me.

At this point, my inner voice was debating. One side secure in the knowledge he was legit and the other side certain that he was another imposter. (This is what online dating does to you). Trust *no one*!

Still unsure, I sent off one last text to check in and see how his day was and if he was feeling better. Not a peep.

This whole thing got me reminiscing back to the prehistoric days when phones were giant blocks attached to walls, and if you were rich and savvy, you might have splurged on an answering machine. But now we're dodging bots, simulations, cat-fishers, pervs and whatever else is lurking out there, while we navigate through mental landmines and trying not to get blown up.

With a bit of trepidation, I called Don the next day with my number blocked, and braced for an awkward conversation. Would he have a Russian accent? Maybe a robotic voice. I was prepared for anything.

But then Don answered. "Hello."

Normal. No voiceovers or radio static.

I took a breath and said "Hello, this is Sharon. I thought I would give you a call and touch base."

There was a few seconds delay and then he said, "Oh, hi, Sharon! How are you doing? It's nice that you called."

Yup, he was real and this was his number and he knew exactly who I was.

So, all my thoughts of being betrayed and spoofed and led astray were all just paranoia. *Justified* paranoia, however, based on my terrible track record with fake profiles.

To make a very long story short the beginnings of our relationship unfolded, then blossomed, got serious, got silly, and sometimes very personal.

Over the next three weeks, we chatted live on the phone, texted for hours upon hours, and tried to set up a day to actually meet. Between me jetting off to Vegas for some wild and crazy girlfriend debauchery (more on this later), and returning with a deadly cold, (because germs and no sleep go hand in hand), we finally set a date in the calendar to meet in the flesh.

And this is where it all fell apart. I guess I should have built up some anticipation first before giving up the ending but what the hell. Let's just spill the tea now.

The in-person (touch, feel, smell) date took place on June 27th at a quaint Italian restaurant in a mutually local neighbourhood. I was dressed in a white tank and white jeans with a funky kimono and matching jewelry. Looking fine.

I got to the restaurant right at the preplanned time (because I'm a bit of a freak that way), but Don was running late. So, I settled in, replied to a few texts on my phone while trying to look casual, ordered a glass of wine, and decided ahead of time what I was going to order. Feeling pretty good and hopeful that he would look as good or even better than his only photo on Tinder.

During my research process earlier, I did find him on his LinkedIn profile and his picture there was pretty dorky. But keeping the faith, I held onto positive thoughts. That said, I did detect nerdiness even during our text and phone conversations, which I chose to ignore – at least at the time.

As I sat there all sexy and ready to impress, perched on my bar stool, I noticed a pint-sized car zooming through the parking lot by the front entrance of the restaurant–almost cartoon style. It was a quick glance but took in a lot of information and immediately said to myself (or maybe out loud – as I may have blacked out for a second), "Oh No! Please don't be him"!

Flash Intake: Very dorky guy, clown hair, wearing a Kelly-green t-shirt (which he alluded to in our early discussions was his favourite color) and glasses.

So, I sat, slightly paralyzed, with him now out of my line of sight, waiting for the verdict. Some time had passed and I finally exhaled, thinking it wasn't him. *Phew! I've been saved.* I returned to playing it cool while I waited.

But I was wrong! The dating gods revealed their sick humour. It was him! And as he bumbled in the front entrance with the gait of a clumsy monkey with rounded shoulders, I stood up, smiled and gave him a welcoming hug. What else could I do? I'm too nice of a person to reject him immediately (as some women have confessed to doing). Don and I already had three weeks of chatting history. And so, I launched my be-nice-and-social persona and made the best of the evening.

It was like many romantic comedies that took a hard left into satire. In-your-face Kelly-green glaring. Clown hair. Smudged glasses as though freshly wiped with a slice of pizza. Kill me now.

Determined to make the best of it (and keeping it totally platonic), I steered the conversation to everything from politics, bathroom habits and my mucus buildup from my recent cold. At this point, I didn't care. I just wanted to eat and get the hell out.

The nerd vibes that I had detected over the phone, pre-date, had been spot on. He was a total Don Knotts, a Gomer Pyle, a Mr. Dress-up, Larry David (with black hair), Mr. Bean all rolled into one not-a-keeper package.

The next day I did do a mini caricature (as any self-respecting artist would do) so I could have a visual for my friends.

Big Clown Poof of Hair – Check.

Slouchy Posture – Check.

Oversized glasses with pepperoni fingerprints – Check.

He wasn't horrid but he was.... Well, he wasn't like his picture. And to be honest, I was pissed off. He didn't represent himself well at all on the dating site and I believe the picture he posted was from about 10 years earlier with a ball cap to hide his hideous hair.

Interestingly, I did not receive a text from him post-date that night saying the usual, "Had a great time, can't wait to see you again," and it was the same the following day—crickets. I guessed he picked up on the fact that I was not interested (perhaps from the mucus talk), even though I ended the date with, "Let's give this another go."

I'm, seriously, too kind!

But then, alas, he did send another text two days later, saying he had been out of town but wanted to confirm his suspicions that indeed there was no connection or chemistry between us. So, he did know. People know. That's what intuition is all about.

Later that day, as I was scrolling through my soon-to-expire Tinder account, his profile popped up in my feed again. It had been updated. A current picture uploaded. One that would definitely tip off the ladies that *he's not all that and a bag of chips.* His hair was frayed out like he lost a battle with a blow dryer, smudgy glasses grasped between his teeth, channeling either a sexy math teacher or a midlife optometrist crisis. It was a poor attempt to look sexy... or studious... or god knows what. But at least it was authentic.

On the bright side though, I really didn't care anymore. The whole finding a man thing was too much work, with a very low success rate and seriously becoming total bullshit! Not worth it.

I left it to the universe to send someone worthy my way–even though it was probably on a break too.

# Chapter 11

Okay... Let's talk Vegas!

Due to the unwelcome interruption of the infamous COVID-19 pandemic in 2020, a milestone birthday trip to *The Strip* with my gal pals had to be put on hold. But now that the cloud of deadly germs had lifted–at least to the point where "you might get sick, but you probably won't die" we finally booked our long-awaited getaway.

Start packing the sequins, sparkle and SPF50.

Enter The Four Blondes!

- Debbie and Judy: sisters by blood, besties by nature
- Sharon and Sharon: the doppelganger duo (yes, two Sharons. Try ordering Starbucks without that getting confusing.)

All natural blondes (yes, we do still exist). All former coworkers at a large radiologist group and still hanging out together.

Debbie, still worked there after 30 plus years, (but retirement was on the near horizon). Meanwhile, the rest of us had gone on to chase other adventures. You must admire the strength of the *Sisterhood.*

Before moving ahead, I must give props to our original Vegas trip back in 2019, which was life changing, at least for me. Not because I won any jackpots, but because I was beginning to step away from a neglectful and crumbling marriage, and desperately needed a sign–any sign–that I was still valid. Still seen.

The Sign? The arena of Magic Mike. Flooded with estrogen and just the right amount of testosterone, we had the perfect cocktail, stirred slowly then shaken. It *was* Magic.

Enter stage left... The one to shake my world. "DRJ", Magic Mike Dancer and saviour, wrapped in tight jeans and glowing abs. I had been truly blessed to have one very fine dancer pay a *lot* of attention to me. I'm not sure if he was even on the main stage that night as he revisited our back table four or five times throughout the evening, each time more stirring and longer than the last. Things got *very* close, very hot and very personal. My muscle memory still sends thank you notes. And unfortunately – or maybe not – that's all I can tell you; because what happens in Vegas, stays in Vegas!

At the end of the performance, as they exited from the stage, he broke off from the chorus line and bee-lined over to me for another unforgettable, albeit sweaty, hug. My *after-show glow* lasted not only for the remainder of the night, but, *seriously*, for months! My friends said they hadn't seen me smile that much in a long while.

I had also slid into DRJ's DMs on Instagram just to keep up with his career–and yeah, I'll admit it, I had created a bond with him, if only in my mind. I also sent him a casual note to let him know that our encounter had brought me back to life and given me the courage to finally move on from a bad marriage. Who needs therapy when a "Magic" dancer can do the trick! I signed off with, "The gang is coming back! Four blonde Canadian gals, ready for another wild night.

To my surprise, he actually wrote back, saying he "would be waiting for us."

I alluded to the fact that he probably didn't remember us (or me) but that was irrelevant. It didn't really matter. I (we) were mostly looking forward to another Magic night, whatever that might have looked like. Spoiler: hot men in rip-away jeans.

Fast forward to 2023 - The Return of the Blondes.

Show night – June 18/23 – we scrambled to get tickets. Lots the day prior and barely any left the night of! We were disappointed because we wanted to get closer to the stage this time around. But alas, we ended up back in the nose-bleeders again, as per our 2019 tour. However, to give some perspective, the theatre is not that big so we could still see quite clearly the sweat, grinding groins, spectacular glutes and incredible muscles from where we sat.

The show started with their usual cheeky banter, teasers sent out to the girls with the expected returned shrieks of excitement as the Emcee promised a fun, sexy night with some hot guys. And on that prompt, the guys filed out onto the stage to do their stuff.

And then, there he was. In the spotlight. My spotlight. My Vegas bond. Emotionally unavailable (and now married, as noted on an IG post), my fantasy man took centre stage.

As the show progressed and *undressed*, with the guys scattering among the sea of hungry, cheering females, "my guy" ascended up to the rafters, with me not expecting to be discovered once again. But miraculously, he appeared. Two feet in front of me!

My whole body ignited, and I could feel this giddy excitement wash over me. What were the chances? The Universe had intervened. As he waited for his cue from the main stage, he turned around and looked right at me. Did he remember me?! All I could think to do was mouth the words, "I texted you!"

He stepped in closer, grabbed my hand and kissed it.

Kissed. It.

I was immediately transported to Magic Mike Heaven. That one moment was all I needed! I was *lit* for the rest of the night. And, yah, it really doesn't take much.

The next moment he was off and back on main stage, my focus completely on him but I was feeling fulfilled. My fantasy was granted.

But then... he came back! Déjà vu!

He returned to our little alcove, gave all my gal pals a quick hug–like a charming rock star on a meet and greet tour–and then came over to me. Maybe he *did* remember me. I wanted to believe he did.

There was a full-on embrace. Hands on, full-body hug. A kiss on my neck and an extra squeeze. A photo was snapped (thanks, Deb!) for posterity. And for a few long seconds, I was the center of his attention.

It was more than I had anticipated as I thought I'd never be found in a sea of screaming women, but I also didn't expect, or require, a repeat of the 2019 connection. That was *special.* That one would stay on the shelf. Preserved. Protected. Untarnished.

Upon our return to Edmonton, I sent DRJ another quick message (along with a few snapshots of him on stage and our sweet hug), thanking him for another magical night and for contributing to our fun evening in Vegas. I told him that life was too short not to express appreciation and that we'd be returning in perhaps another year, or two. Again, he replied, "I'll be waiting for you and you are appreciated." Short and sweet.

My takeaway is never underestimate human connection, even if it's staged. It *can* make a difference.

Meanwhile, I was doing my best not to come off as some creeper or stalker or someone who's a bit psycho! Hopefully, I stuck the landing somewhere in the charming and self-aware zone."

Will we make a trip back next year? I felt like we still had another Blonde Adventure in us, so time will tell.

But in the year that followed, I discovered the infamous love of my Magic Mike life had retired. Yup, he had boxed up his breakaways and boots for good... Or at least for a different type of stage. Happily married and, perhaps, plans for a family. I say, good for him! I've got fun memories to take with me and stories that start with, "Did I ever tell you about the time...."

After the Vegas trip and recovering from a bad cold, not to mention the lingering bad taste from *Don the Circus Clown*, I decided to cast my line back into the murky waters of "Plenty of Fish." Yup, that site is still around – for those who know it.

I had used the site many years earlier, and actually met my third husband there in 2008. He was a keeper for a while, but I tossed him back into the pond 12 years later. From what I understand he is now swimming happily in a new lady's pool. I've met her. She's nice.

# Chapter 12

So, Plenty of Fish (POF) proved to be much more exciting. The guys were a tad better looking and more responsive. However, I knew not to pay this time or get locked into a monthly subscription.

The only downside was I couldn't see "likes." If a guy hit the little heart sign to indicate interest, I would not be able to see him unless I coughed up some serious cash. Not happening this time, sister.

Meanwhile, I had over 200 likes which just sat there dormant. Interestingly enough, I was not even curious. Why? Because I specifically stated in the first sentence in my profile, "*I cannot see likes, please send me a message*."

If they couldn't grasp or understand that straightforward guidance, then–BOOM!—gone. Automatically weeded out. Thank you.

So, here's what happened over a two-week period, post Vegas...

First up was Lance, who showed interest. Texted a bit and set up a date to meet quickly. Bonus points for that. However, he cancelled and rebooked the meeting to the next day, at a Starbucks, as he said he got too busy. So, we regrouped to meet at a different location. I went to said location and waited... and waited. After about 20 minutes I texted "Hey where are you?" He said he was waiting at another Starbucks in a different neighbourhood, and after 15 minutes decided to leave. I offered to wait for him if he could head my way, but no reply. Crickets again. I gave it 10 more minutes, just in case, then said, "Screw it."

I closed the deal via text: "Thanks for wasting my day, asshole." That seemed to trigger a response but now he was trying to blame me for not checking in sooner since I had his number. Blah, blah, blah...

Was he really at the wrong location? Did he care to apologize and rebook again? Nah.

Lance—gone and blocked!

In the dating site world, if anyone pisses you off, you block them. No hesitation. It's law.

Next, we had a Gord, a Todd, a Steven, a Shane and, very briefly, a Liam (no notes on him, clearly forgettable). Then I had a David.

Out of all of them, I was still corresponding with out-of-town Todd, who was much younger than me and probably just looking for a hook up. But he liked to golf and was very upfront about his needs and wants. Convo was light and fun, so he was entertaining if nothing else. Maybe an option for an FWB. If I got that desperate.

Steven was an asshole right from the start. Said he was moving to Edmonton or Calgary from Minnesota and needed a realtor, of which I kindly provided him a name and number to call. He actually contacted the realtor and when I followed up with "How's it going", he hit me with, "Well, I can't buy a house if I'm from another country." (Seemed citizen-red-tape logical to me).

So, I said, "Well, good luck!"

He snapped back, "what do you mean good luck?!! I'm angry."

OoooKaaaay then.

Backed away slowly and... Steven—blocked!

Next, Shane...

Zzzzzz. Oops! Sorry, I just fell asleep. Real snooze-fest. I would text about five or six sentences, ask him a question or share a highlight from my day. Shane's best? A maximum of five words if I was lucky. One time he really opened up emotionally and said, "I like you."

Whoa, Shane, slow your roll. Shane—blocked!

I almost feel like I should have a big red button with a buzzer I can press and have them fall through a trap door in the floor. How satisfying would that be? Add a dramatic game show sound effect—*Waw-Waw*—and the dude disappears into the abyss.

Moving on to David. He let me know right from the get-go that he was working in another Province (he was a hyperbolic welder, which apparently is a real thing and not just a fancy sci-fi job term), and wouldn't be back in Edmonton until August. I assured him I was in no rush and could just chat. So chat we did, in great detail. For a day or two, and then—POOF! Gone. Not even a pile of ashes. I guess David wasn't really into it after all. Or he had a major mood swing. Surprisingly, he resurfaced a few days later but only to take in some air before re-submerging. And that's pretty much where he stayed. Stealth Mode. Radar, undetected. Most likely zapped by his *hyperbolic* tool. David—blocked!

Then there was good old Gordy! Took my chance on this one as I wasn't too sure about his photos. Confusing combo of kinda young and kinda too old all at the same time. At least he posted one of him and not just his car. Or dog.

I took the plunge anyway and sent a message to which he replied. Short chat session and then coffee date set up quickly. Good sign and less wasted time. It also means they're more sincere.

And so, we met at–you guessed it—Starbucks!

*Hmmm, I'm thinking that somehow Starbucks could cash in on this dating phenomenon; perhaps "First Date Frequent Flyer" points. Definitely marketing opportunities there!*

Anyway, Gord and I sat for little over an hour and found out we had lots in common, grew up in the same neighbourhood, knew the local bands from our era and shared some personal stories about our struggles, our kids and life in general. And because I'm such a bubbly, funny and kind person (and humble), I could tell he felt a connection. But while he was already envisioning me in his bedroom, I was envisioning a quick and gentle exit. To add to the ick factor, his mannerisms and features reminded me of my dad. And that's just a bad thing all around.

The coffee date finally wrapped up and he walked me out to my car. We made some awkward small talk and then I leaned in to give him a hug. It seemed the polite thing to do. But instead, I was overtaken with slobbering lips lunging towards me. I jumped back a bit and said, "Oh, I wasn't expecting a kiss!" to which he planted another one on me. This time, I'm thinking Golden Retriever vibe or that dog from Turner and Hooch. Certainly not appreciated.

Apparently, he was undeniably attracted to me.

I decided to blame it on my bubbly personality, which can easily be mistaken for intense interest and flirtation. It's a curse, really.

Many days passed and after declining a lunch date with him the next day by saying, "I was busy until Sunday," I didn't hear back from him until a full week later. I thought, and hoped, that he had just gone away.

But alas, he had my phone number, which I'd stupidly given to him in the parking lot. It was more of a buffer as you *never* reject a man in person. It can get nasty, quickly! Reject by text only.

He called, and we chatted more about life, kids and struggles and then wrapped it up. The next day, he contacted me, surprisingly via the dating site and not my phone, asking if I still wanted to talk. And this is where it got ugly(ish). It was time to drop the bomb, come clean, and let him know how I felt.

Me: Hey, I think you're a great guy, but I don't think there's anything romantically connecting for me. Nothing personal of course but you either feel it or you don't. And I doubt you're looking for just friends. ☺ "

Gord: I agree. I don't find you attractive at all. I thought maybe friendship. But probably not. Good luck!

"*I don't find you attractive at all*?!" Ouch. There's some hurt and childish rebuttal for you; *wounded male ego, dead ahead!* I mean, OMG! We met on a dating site and had coffee once. And we're going to resort to insults?

Only because I sometimes like to have the last word before I Block, I replied, "Sorry, Gord. I enjoyed talking to you but I didn't feel a spark that I personally need to continue. But since you find me absolutely hideous, then I guess there is not an issue. All the best."

Gord was... (say it with me) ...BLOCKED!

Over the next several weeks, the dating scene died down a bit. Not too many messages coming my way, but still a steady trickle of *likes* that I couldn't see.

No great loss, though. If they couldn't read the **bolded** instructions at the top of my dating profile that says, "I CANNOT SEE LIKES, PLS MSG", then they were basically weeding themselves out by their own stupidity. Saved me time, so—Thanks!

That said, I did discover a little hack that lets you *see* who isn't worthy of you. If you touch and hold the small, blurred out thumbnail of the guy that likes you, the bubble expands and you can actually see the picture.

So far, no George Clooney, Brad Pitt or Jason Momoa types had slipped through the POF filters. Thank God. Can you imagine accidentally missing that opportunity only because you refused to front a bit of cash? Tragic!

However, one creeper (and obviously fake profile) did manage to crawl out of the woodwork.

He looked potentially promising, so I sent a message. *"Just saying a quick hello for today. Drop me a note back if interested."*

His reply? (*Summarized only to save you from reading too much garbage.*) "Aww angel, it's my pleasure meeting you pretty."

Bad grammar aside, we hadn't met so there should be no *pleasure*.

*"I'm sure you are doing good and having a great morning at the moment or probably in bed snuggling with your pillow...."*

Yuck! The last thing I want this guy to be visualizing is me in bed. Doing anything!

"*My name is Peter and I'm very new to dating online...*"

Sure, you are, Peter... suuure you are.

*"I really like your smile and you're a cool beautiful woman. Are you truly single and ready to mingle?"*

"Ready to mingle?" What is this – 1995? Cheese and cringe all in one icky ball.

*"Have you ever dated a Frenchman before?"*

Good lord, spare me! And, yes, I was married to one!

*"However, I will suggest you should grab a plate of meal at the Normand restaurant, fabulous dishes, always makes my mouth yummy anytime I'm in your area."*

I'm sorry, what? Is this even a sentence? "Plate of meal?" "Mouth yummy?" Time to shut this one down!

My final words, "Yes, I was married to a French guy and he didn't sound as creepy as you."

And you already know what happened next.

Red Button... POOF! Blocked.

Then we had Karl.

*(Quick side note: These excerpts are for pure comedic purposes and a closer look into the messed-up world of online dating).*

I sent Karl a short note just to say hello.

He soon replied, *"How are you doing today, Sharon. Thank you for the friendship you have offered; rest assured that I'll treasure it in my heart. Your smile looks like you are happy all the time. I will appreciate it. Tell me more about yourself."*

Okay, first red flag: fake vibes from his grammar and syntax. Probably AI generated. And the "treasure it in my heart?" Classic Harlequin romance crap.

My response was, *"Hello Karl, I am only saying hi at this time. Friendship MAY have been offered later but meanwhile there's no reason to treasure anything in your heart."*

BLOCKED.

NEXT! (By now you've probably grasped the meaning behind the title of this book).

Having taken a break for several weeks to attend to other personal matters, such as my art career, which was still in the early stages, but showing promise, and guiding, rather unsuccessfully, one of my adult children in matters of the heart (again), I returned back to the flimsy façade of the online dating world, only because *real life* was still not generating any potential suitors.

The lead for this one... Ian.

I always keep first contact short, as there's no benefit to spilling your guts about yourself until they show interest in getting to know you.

Ian took about a week to get back to me but he did. And he sounded normal! (by some definition...)

Easy going, intelligent conversation went back and forth. We talked about BBQing for a while. Then he said that he was intrigued about me and suggested that we meet. Good sign and saved endless text banter that leads nowhere.

I felt very positive about this one and was actually visualizing a future with him and all the fun adventures we'd have. (No judgment please. This was just a knee-jerk reaction and renewed excitement to someone who *seemed* to be a genuine, sincere person).

Since I felt relief and joy, I suggested that we exchange phone numbers (which I rarely do) and he agreed it would be a great idea so we could set up a date to meet.

*And this is where it fell apart.*

(Do I even need to foreshadow ANY of this going forward?)

The number he gave was an area code in Nevada, and when I diligently performed the reverse number search, it did not line up with any "Ian's." So, I quickly wrote back to confirm that he actually lived in Edmonton in case there was some confusion.

He responded, "Yah, it's not a local number, but I live in Edmonton. Just send me a text with your name so I do not forget."

*(Obviously, this guy has a spreadsheet of all the ladies he's misleading/ deceiving).*

When I asked again, what part of Edmonton do you live in, the conversation ended. Time passed. No reply.

And there went my little Cinderella fantasy bubble of a *happily ever after* life with Ian. Pop...fizzle...

As hard as my *Singles Mingles* lady's group tried (which I mentioned earlier) to sniff out suitable, quality men, we had yet to come up with anything remotely close. Even in the stark light of day, and the dimmest light of night, we failed.

- Sports bars – Steeeerike!
- Singles Nights – Still Single.
- Street festivals – Only thing getting action: the foot long hotdogs.
- Bike/car races – Just the sound of men speeding away.
- Beer tents – Kegs of bros who peaked long ago.

Inevitably, we resorted back to trolling, scrolling and blocking men on Tinder, Bumble, Match, POF... and the list goes on.

I remember a time when I was much younger (which could be key to this whole observation), when I could go out with friends to a bar, lounge, party, picnic... whatever have you, and find a guy within an hour to date, go party with, hook-up with, even marry (in a few cases). It was easy as washing your hands and putting on another swipe of lipstick. But now? OMG! I couldn't find a man to even go to a show with if my life depended on it.

What the hell happened? Are *all* the great guys happily married, never to be released out into the wild again? It was a sobering (and somewhat hopeless) thought that many of my single buds shared. We couldn't give up because the alternative...well, it's not what we wanted. We know we don't *need* a man, but we would like one.... Please?

After taking yet another break, I latched on to a guy named Scott, who lived an hour outside of my city–so not ideal. We chatted a bit and he was the first one to suggest we meet in person, sooner rather than later. This is a big green flag in the online world. And he seemed normal.

So normal that we met up for our first date at IKEA. (I think that translates to "common sense" in Swedish. And maybe *build* an actual relationship with a pinewood foundation–and an Allen key).

We started with the ever-popular Swedish meatball café for the usual get-to-know-you chat, then wandered through a maze of Kleppstad, Slattum and Tarva furniture, only to get turned around and lost in the kitchen and bath dioramas. Checking out a shower stall, a small flirty waist-touch moment happened and I felt a spark of chemistry.

In the end, I bought napkins, he bought lunch.

It was a fun afternoon. I could tell via body language, he was interested. And I was struck by a flutter of butterflies. I had almost forgot what that felt like.

We left the IKEA world of stick furniture, said our goodbyes and exchanged phone numbers.

It was time to... *"Start the car! Start the car!" (referencing an old IKEA commercial).*

After a few texts throughout the week and a tentative plan to meet on the following Saturday (after I returned from my *mom mission* in Vancouver to visit my son) we reconnected and setup a date.

One that morphed by the hour from a football game to dinner on the weekend to hitting a golf course with one of his buddies, where I would be the third wheel. (Nice... or maybe not.) Nonetheless, I had been dying and trying to get out golfing all summer and this would probably be my last chance. (My ladies "WOW Golf Group", was barely *putting* along...) So, I said yes to "Tee and FORE-play." Even if I had to share him.

My ever-punctual self showed up half hour before tee time, (which is basic golf etiquette). He, however, arrived a few minutes before we were set to tee-off. Slightly annoying. Already *flubbing* the ball, so to speak, before we even got started. If he kept this behaviour up, he'd be over par much sooner than later.

A few minutes later, after he arrived, so did his buddy, Gord. And *his* buddy, Ray and *his* buddy Tom (or whatever their names were). So now I was third wheeling in a five-some. How romantic.

I also had a 7:00 date with a gal pal, which undoubtedly, I'd be late for, so I had to let her know.

In the end, we had a great game of golf and had some good laughs. It was all very buddy/buddy/buddy and I probably did more flirting with, Gord, than with Scott. But Scott was not a golfer per se, so maybe he was focussing to hold his ground with his more experienced teammates.

His clubs were mismatched and probably some were older than he was, so he wasn't out to impress or be serious about making par. Nonetheless, even with us sharing a golf cart, he never once leaned into me or touched me or contributed to my tasteless, yet flirty golf/sex innuendos that always seem to come so naturally when you're talking about balls, strokes, holes, etc.

On the bright side, I golfed my best game yet (like ever), so I was very happy about that. But since I had to putt and run back to the city, we said our goodbyes quickly and we agreed to text later to make a new plan for dinner.

The next day, he got back to me to say he was crazy busy for the rest of the weekend, to which I replied, "Well you're the busy one, so I'll leave this in your court to get back to me for dinner, if you're interested."

At this point, I wasn't sure if he *was* interested as three days passed and still no word.

A week later, he resurfaced—kinda. He said he was free in the upcoming week but then bailed due to work (which was part Zamboni driver and part septic tank business owner). Already on thin ice (pun intended), I began to take him at his earlier word that he was "not dating material." Ya think?

I left it on the table, so to speak, and extended a wilting olive branch to him, noting that if you're ever *not* busy, drop me a note. But like the others, Scott, disappeared into the dating abyss. Or perhaps got sucked up by his septic tank hose.

Meanwhile, in early October, I had a very handsome gent, named Mark, reach out to me from the POF dating site (which I've renamed as "Plenty of Fakes" and/or "Plenty of F*** ups". Either way, a losing battle.) Despite the odds, he seemed *normal.* We immediately hit it off and he was so normal it was scary. We text chatted for about half an hour when I finally came to the realization this guy was real and quite interested. He even gave me his home address and last name.

Feeling safe, I caved and gave him my phone number. Within minutes, we were texting outside the restrictive walls of POF. After about 20 minutes, he asked me to call him so we could talk and save our fingers from callouses. And from there, we talked for another good hour, laughing, vibing and making a connection.

He was considerably younger than me (in his 50s), but confessed he had always liked older women. And I, of course, always preferred younger men. So perfect again!

I don't think I had connected this easily with a guy on so many levels so quickly, so my happy endorphins were running rampant.

I was thinking in my *fairy tale female mind* this could be the One! We went on discussing my artistic skills, and even talked about the possibility of me doing a painting for him and what colors would work in his living room (he even sent me a pic). Again, the conversation just flowed and I was falling for every wonderful word that came out of his mouth.

The next few days, he texted me, "good morning, sunshine" and "hello beautiful," and said he was looking forward to meeting me on the Thanksgiving Monday (which was to be at an art gallery or even Home Sense so we could look at potential art styles). The last text I got from him was "text me later when you get home from your family dinner".

And that's where it ended! Radio silence.

Oof!

Thinking this couldn't be how it ended, I sent him two follow-up texts to see if he was still available and if plans had changed. But no response. And for some reason, this one felt like a sucker punch!

Naturally, this led to a few frantic texts to an empathetic girlfriend, who was a newly found friend from the last few months. We clicked nicely on many levels and were going through the same basic shit with men, mostly via the dating sites. Her "fuck men" replies were exactly the kind of emotional CPR I needed. This one had really taken me down a notch and I needed all the help I could get.

It was crazy to realize that I hadn't even *met* this guy yet and I was already feeling tinges of "we just broke up" heart pains. Believe me when I say that dating is not for the faint of heart. And as you get older, it just gets worse (in some ways), and you start to lose hope. You wonder if your senior years will be spent alone. No romance, no laughs over morning coffee or sharing a cocktail at sunset. Human beings weren't designed to live solo – unless that really is your vibe. We thrive on love, companionship, human touch and all those other beautifully messy things.

On the bright side (however dim it may seem at times), I'd reached a point in my life where I valued myself more and wouldn't settle for mediocrity and disrespect. I am very happy living on my own and truly have no desire to remarry or live with a man (unless it's for financial reasons). My happiness comes from me and only me. How I respond and react is key for a sound mind and holding peace within myself. However, this will and does get tested and poked every so often and I do have my low moments – which I continually must rise from.

*I know I've written variations of this revelation throughout this book, but it bears repeating... if only to help keep my own spirits lifted through the writing process.*

On the other hand our married counterparts have a different perspective. They often question the motives and mindsets of us single ladies. Even if they are happily married, they are baffled as to why we willingly jump into the chaos and emotional landmines that come with dating. Honestly, I get it. Sometimes we do think the grass is greener on the other side– and has fewer dandelions–but only for a short while.

There are definitely perks to living on your own. No rules! No one watching you eat ice cream for breakfast and Capt'n Crunch for dinner. You can be as filthy or as neat as you like. You can fart, burp and snore without worrying who's in ear's reach, and you can watch all the chick flicks and reality garbage as much as you want. No judgment is ever made.

But at the end of the day... and a few months/years of lonely nights, solo vacations (if you're even taking them) and no one to cuddle up with on the couch (cuz our pets can only provide so much), you do realize you do want, and perhaps need, someone romantically partnered with you. (Just not living with you).

And this is what keeps us pounding the pavement, searching in dusty corners, swiping and dragging ourselves through pathetic dating sites, and hanging on to that frayed string of hope that maybe, just maybe, he's just around the next corner.

*At this time, I would like to thank all the guys who have provided me with so much misery, laughs, WTF's and endless inspiration. Your nonsense is fueling this book. I think I only need another 60 pages or more before I hit Publish!*

Moving on from men who could not be trusted on any level, I made a date with one man I could. My doctor. Time for my annual physical.

Nothing major going on but I always like to stay proactive when it comes to my health. Since I didn't have any daunting illnesses or pain that disrupted my life, we had a much more animated and casual conversation than usual. Almost bordering on flirtatious, but not quite crossing the line. I mean, he *is* a professional. Married with kids and probably *much* younger than me. Not to say he isn't handsome as all hell. It just makes my visits more enjoyable. However, talking about poop and lady part issues does feel a bit embarrassing. He often reassures me "It's all part of the job." But still... *Awkward!*

Meanwhile, back on the exam table, as he reached out to do a standard lymph node check under the arm pits, my body immediately folded in on itself. I am so ridiculously ticklish that any contact with that area will be rejected. I scrunched up my face like a child getting a needle and tried to endure the *attack*. It was futile and he thought it was hilarious. "You made my day", he said.

From there the appointment just took on a silly, slightly unprofessional turn. I even blurted out–after confessing I was still unemployed, financially struggling and still single—"Do you know any single men?" Yep, I said it! As the words escaped out of my mouth, I knew I had crossed the line. He did laugh but asserted that he wasn't offering a dating service.

In the end, I did see that I got him flustered and his train of thought did go off the rails a bit. It was funny but at least it was a highlight of my afternoon. And apparently his. Prior to my appointment, one of my friends jokingly suggested I batt my new eyelash extensions during my visit just to spice things up. I think they did their job.

Post doctor's exam, I headed off to Michaels (the giant craft haven) to pick up a few items I needed for an upcoming art show. While I wandered through the labyrinth of aisles, my son called me to bring me up to date on the ever changing, ever stressful fabric of his life. But it was all good and positive. He seemed to see light at the end of the tunnel, some possible job prospects, which may have assisted him in also finding a place to live, and, finally, an opportunity to make some quick cash helping a friend move from Edmonton to Vancouver. All very positive, so I took the win and so did he.

Moving on, and back to dating traumas, I had deleted "Zamboni Scott"; "No Art for You, Mark" and many others not worthy of my time or my heart. But being the trooper (or sucker) that I am, I moved on to Kyle. Or someone who said his name was Kyle.

He came in hot. Funny and flirtatious and not short on the compliments. (As I typed this, hindsight being the bitch she is, I started to see what I didn't see before). *Too* flirtatious. *Too* excited to meet me. Too "I'm the perfect guy for you" and vice versa. Red flags justa flapping!

But my optimism prevailed. He seemed sincere, his English and grammar were good, he knew lots about Edmonton and the area I lived in, and he wasn't 500 miles up north working on an oil rig. Apparently he lived in a ritzy neighbourhood about 10 minutes from me and was already inviting me over to share drinks in his hot tub. Of course, I quickly shut that down and suggested a more public venue. He laughed and made light of it claiming he was just joking around.

Part two of his sketch ball script: he asked if I knew any single ladies for his buddy, who was obviously hanging out with him. (If you can't see where this is going by now, then you are as blind as I was). Yup, his friend, the *dentist,* 46 years old.

But since my calendar was wide open, I put on my dating blinders and agreed to meet him at a local pub in a mutual proximity neighbourhood at 8:00. I got myself all dolled up, looking pretty good with the extra bonus of having a great hair day! My skin looked like it had been kissed with an Instagram filter and my new lash extensions were living up to my expectations and monetary investment!

I left my house with confidence and arrived promptly at 8:00pm, (as I do) and ordered a glass of red wine while I waited for my hot tub Romeo to grace me with his presence and full undivided attention. I caught up on a few text messages, read some emails and watched the minutes tick by.

8:10. No Kyle. Still hopeful.

8:20. Still No Kyle.

By 8:30, *hope* was packing its bag and halfway out the door.

I tried messaging him, through the app, but got only crickets." As I watched a few more cars slow their pace in the parking lot, thinking the next one might be him, I finally resigned myself to the fact that I had been scammed. Stood up. Played. I could see that this had all been orchestrated by some asshole(s) on the dating site to mess with women like me. I was angry, of course, but I finally finished my wine (thankfully it was only $5) and headed back home at 9:00.

Fuckin' men! Or more specifically, fuckin' men scammers!

Rather than let this piece of scum ruin my otherwise great day, I let it go. However, as a seasoned vigilante of on-line dating, I reported his profile to POF stating this person was a scammer and needed to be booted off quicker than a drunk uncle at a wedding. With great satisfaction on some level, POF got back to me to say they reviewed his profile and he is now banned. I felt better knowing I did my part keeping our virtual streets safe and clean from the likes of dickheads like "Kyle" and their spawn.

Next!

Although it's not obvious in *book time*, I took a break from writing (and dating apps) for about a month. With the dating swipes still on hold, I could no longer bear the fake, insincere, ignorant ramblings and lost souls that resided within those digital dungeons.

Honestly, I was becoming depressed and beginning to lose respect for *all* men. It was not healthy or helpful when you're trying to remain a hopeful romantic. So, I quit. Cold turkey.

The first hour was a bit tricky because I had taken away an addiction of sorts, checking emails, getting a little dopamine hit when there was a message (like Pavlov's dog) and sometimes being rewarded with someone who could string two sentences together about a somewhat interesting topic.

But by the next day, something beautiful happened. I remembered my life. The one I knew, cherished and appreciated. And, consequently, my focus redirected itself to more important needs. Jobs, money, health and peace of mind.

And to that end, in the month of November 2023, I finally found a job—two actually! Within the first week (as per my usual Feast or Famine lifestyle), I got two part-time jobs, a new kitten (*more about that later*) and then proceeded to put my back out! Arghh! Always the Ying and the Yang.

Due to this unscheduled disability, it was very difficult to look after a tiny kitten, bending over to feed her, pick her up, clean her litter box, chase her off furniture, and all the other little joys a kitten brings with it. My timing is often not great, and this again would be a prime example of how my life usually unfolds. Honestly, I should be studied.

As for the new jobs. The first one was pursued more in unfiltered desperation. My bank account was down to nickels and I was days away from enlisting with the Mob. (Ancestry states I'm 9% Italian. And, hey, *"I know people..."*). Either that, or sign up on Only Fans, profiting from my feet or whatever *modest* kink might be out there. I always like to put my best foot forward in life and this would be a *baby step* in that direction. (Sorry, that pun was low-hanging fruit, buy I regret nothing). Not to judge, but women are out there making bank selling various body parts to survive–maybe even thrive!

In the end, I chose a more righteous path. My second job offer was one of those bubbly ladies in the liquor store giving out wine samples to the pre-inebriated public. I did have a passion for chatting with people, I drink wine, and I thought this would be a great way to meet men! I often have ulterior motives for some of my actions and this was one of them. A little wine, mixed with flirtation and a phone number or two? Sign me up.

Within a few days, I got offered another job. Like a real job with benefits (or so I thought), great office hours and coworkers. However, it wasn't *exactly* like that (cue up pending danger music here). I was working from home, part-time (9-1:00) in the comfort of my little office/art studio. No super early mornings, no battling traffic or dodging formidable snowbanks. Just my morning tea, a roguish cat and my laptop. Bliss.

As for my Zoom-only boss? Mid-30's, still young but was the big cheese of his own company.

To me, this felt like a dream job. The industry was right up my alley and perhaps through connections made, as a result of being the main office gal, I might meet a handsome and available man based on the type of clientele it would attract. I'm thinking nicely tailored blazer, good teeth and a decent cash flow.

I know, I'm relentless, but the underlying theme of this book *is* How to Find a Man (of quality). Or, maybe, more precisely, How to *Survive* in the Dating Jungle. We could look at it as one large anthropology experiment to find the elusive fully-evolved man. So, in principle, I'm doing research.

The job training all took place via Google Meets. The first day was definitely challenging, but so far, so good. The downside about working from home: you're alone all day, no human interaction and in my case, trying to keep a crazy ass kitten from destroying the place.

This is where the side job of wine-peddling swoops in like a hero with a corkscrew, to provide the social balance. But before I get to the wine boss (which feels vaguely Mafioso) let's talk about.... pussy.

Kittens, specifically. Kittens with weapons of mass destruction. Kittens with attitude and a flair for drama. Kittens who will push the limits, with the momentum of a toddler on Red Bull, and then rewrite the limits. I could go on, but I'll refrain.

I think those who have adopted and raised a kitten can relate to all of this. We endure their antics because when they aren't completely ballistic, or scaling curtains like Spiderman, they are these sweet, furry little balls of fluff, purring like a luxury sports car with little nose kisses.

*My* little she-devil, named Bella (aka "Bella the Destroyer"), and often pronounced as one long anguished cry "NO BELLA!", was one such creature.

She was still in training, which meant I was still in training. It was painful. My house looked like it was staged by a paranoid exorcist: orange peels scattered like landmines (cats don't like citrus); tin foil on chairs (the feel and sound freaks them out), spray bottles ready to blast and plastic barb wire under furniture, aka, plastic pokey mats.

According to my Google Search, cats are supposed to hate all of these strategies.

According to Bella, Google is full of shit!

She welcomed them all. Orange peels were just more playthings to toss around; tin foil was a mirror to admire her cuteness in; and the spray bottle was a mist of Evian to freshen up. At this point, I wouldn't have been surprised if she was laundering money in... well, the laundry room.

But as she tore through my house like a furry little tornado, we had bonded and I loved her....

"BELLA! NOOOOOOO!" Sigh...

# Chapter 13

Okay, so bottoms up (no reference to dating, booty calls or regrettable encounters). We now venture into the world of wine. Not just any ordinary wine, but an elixir made of berries, flowers and honey. A beautiful "marriage" between a garden fairy and a beekeeper. Magical.

Then there was the *wine boss*... anything but magical.

If you looked up "effective communication," his name would be missing. However, if you looked under "chaos, vague directions, ghosting and deflection," his name would have been bolded and underlined.

From day one, he texted out instructions with dates that didn't match, incomplete sentences and two word replies to my three (very relevant) questions. Not an uncommon problem amongst those who don't take time to read, comprehend and respond.

I quickly cracked the code. One question per hour, maybe with multiple choice answers, and reconfirming details.

Nonetheless, I bumped along the rocky winey road and did my pop-ups at various liquor stores, like a bubbly, chatty peddler selling her wares. Travel time was usually 30-40 minutes with a set up time of about 40 minutes. So, it took up a big chunk of my day along with the 4-hour shifts. Glamourous? Not really but I enjoyed the people watching (and judging), the occasional flirting with some middle-aged dad, and of course imbibing the remaining sample shots left untasted.

But the man-in-charge himself? Kind of a tool. Sorry to say but true. During one very "wordless" chat, I asked if I'd be working *every* Friday and Saturday or just some of them, he never responded. Then later, when I asked if I could be excused for an upcoming Friday due to a doctor's appointment, he went into a full-blown WTF meltdown over text, like full CAPS LOCK energy. He accused me of going back on my word that I'd be available for Fridays and Saturdays. Never once had he mentioned *every single one* was mandatory. Nor had he specified in his imaginary employee handbook there would be no exceptions.

Then he went off the rails, throwing around simple math like an angry toddler with a calculator.

"You've cancelled three dates and only worked six stores... that's like half!"

OMG. Like, fuck right off. (Sorry, but my story needs swears; it's part of the healing process).

The reality? I missed the very first assignment because I'd hurt my back (didn't want to expose my weak spot too early), so I said it was a family emergency–me being the "family." He was still salty about it. But math-wise, I'd already worked *eight* stores, and I was only *asking* for *one* Friday off.

I sucked it up and offered to "work around my doctor's appointment" just to minimize the tantrum. And suddenly he was fine. Amazing how people calm down when you pretend their nonsense is rational.

Meanwhile, he rarely respected *my* time. Prime example: one day I arranged to meet him at his house to pick up wine supplies, at a specific time. I drove over, rang his doorbell like a responsible adult, and he wasn't even home! Standing out in the freezing cold, with a few more attempts at the doorbell, I was ready to give up. Just as I was ready to text him, his wife showed up (thank God for women!) After quickly evaluating the situation, she rolled her eyes and said, "Yeah, he's really bad with time."

Ya think?!

# Chapter 14

By mid-December, my line graph was displaying that dating sites weren't working (which were on hold anyway until early Spring), the liquor stores weren't bringing in nicely dressed gentlemen to buy their $100 bottles of Scotch, and the attempts at hanging out in sports bars or meeting men via my other job were all falling short. And even with a divorce rate of approximately 45%, not one of my friends or family knew a decent man that was solo. Begs the questions of Who, What, Where and Why?!

Back to book time where Earth's rotations stand still. I returned to assess where I stood in the dark abyss of dating and dating sites.

I probably mentioned that I torched all my dating apps into a hot, smoldering pile of shit, never to return. And so far, at that point in time, I had stayed away. My new work-from-home job, although now three months in, had been keeping me quite busy, but I was quite happy to slam my laptop shut at 1:00 sharp. However, how can I get a book written if I'm curled up on my couch, yelling at my cat? Or more specifically, cleaning toppled plant pots, rewiring my electric fence system around said plants (kidding of course) and wondering why the hell I'm putting myself through all of this!

Still, the lingering truth was: I didn't have a boyfriend to cuddle and/or yell at. I did, however, sense another *Next* approaching. Soon. In fact, it would be right around the corner, quite literally.

"Thanks to good timing, a little luck, and maybe some patience, I did stumble across a guy on "Facebook Dating". I never really deleted that one as it's a freebie from Zuckerberg's vision of world domination, abducting our minds and keeping us addicted to the social media mess. So, it had stayed open.

And through that open door, entered Jacob.

To my benefit (or maybe not), he literally, lived down the street. We had been talking and texting on the phone for two days straight. Like every hour. I'm like, "Wow! Who is this rare male of the species giving me his full attention, and hanging on my every word and every joke?

In fact, I started to wonder... "Have I latched on to–or more specifically—has *he* latched onto me in some kind of very needy way?" I chose to ignore the tiny voice in my head and see how this played out.

I was being overly optimistic, and I got a bit caught up in all the attention, excitement, lust, and silliness of early flirting. Of course, we all know that at some point, those cute habits that make you think he's adorable become the same habits that make you ask yourself, "Why the hell does he keep doing that?!" Oh, the joys of coupledom.

It only took a few days for him to start raising the RED FLAGS and a new buzzword entered my vocabulary. *Love Bombing.* I did a Google search just to confirm he qualified. We had a match.

Nonetheless, we were having a lot of laughs and easy conversations, so a date night was set. Time to meet this attentive creature in person. Since he lived just two blocks away and we practically shared a mailbox, I allowed him to pick me up. In my defense, we had a solid five hours of phone time so it made him less strange.

So, I dolled myself up, highlighted the brows, trimmed the chin hairs (because... dignity!) and put on something sexy but still subtle. The big reveal was coming up and soon we'd really know if we were a match.

Pick up time. The moment we'd both find out if the phone vibes translated into in-person chemistry.

I was confident, curious and exfoliated.

As his car pulled up, my brain kicked into overdrive, processing everything in nanoseconds—observing, assessing, and recalibrating the imagery coming towards me. The car was a tad beat up, but not judging. I see him looking at me, but I'm trying to look cool, aloof. *Don't make eye contact yet.* Open the door... climb in and notice cleanliness. Passed.

Then I glanced over.

Oh.

That's one very large man! Totally caught off guard by his significant girth, I tried not to stare, thankful that thought bubbles don't pop up over our heads. Instead, I mentally smacked myself and said "Sharon... don't be superficial."

However, from the neck up, passable. Handsome enough, cute smile (but later noticed – missing a tooth). He finally chimed in with, "WOW, you're even better looking in person," and stared at me a bit longer than was comfortable. I was flattered but unfortunately, I couldn't find the words to reciprocate. Should I say, "Thank you?" or fake a "You too?"

Nonetheless, we drove off to our destination and got settled in a booth. Conversation flowed easily, and I maintained focus on his face and not what was south of it. About 10 minutes into the date, he reached across the table to hold my hands and then repeatedly told me how beautiful I was. With these huge puppy dog eyes, I could see I was his sun and his moon.

I did my best to focus on the positives as he did have a fun personality and cute(ish) features. He genuinely seemed excited just to be around me. And admittedly, it was an ego boost for me.

But as the alcohol flowed with a few glasses of wine, and possibly a shooter or two, bad decisions were made–at least from my perspective. Bad. Bad. Decisions.

Putting his physical attributes aside, I decided there would be a second date. I was determined not to be swayed by his lack of a six pack, which was more of a Molson Mound. And trust me when I say, it was not your average beer belly; it was literally an obstacle. The kind you mentally plan around. "So, if we hug, I'll go left...?"

I thought if anything would deter me from this relationship, it would have to be something other than a physical issue. Like character flaws or emotional immaturity. And, lo and behold, the red flags began to wave.

Besides the love bombing behaviour, which included being overly attentive, compliments over the roof, moving way too fast with the affection and "Are we going steady yet?", it was the constant texting every hour, the three phone calls a day and the reactions from him when I didn't respond to a text message fast enough. How dare I take longer than 10 minutes? I'd just get another text along the lines of "Oh, we're not talking now?!"

Seriously, dude! I was buying cat litter. Relax!

It got to the point, that every time my phone would ping with a new message from him, I would cringe. Not a good sign for the beginning of a relationship.

During one of our conversations after our second date, he told me he'd shown my photo to his buddies at his local watering hole, *The Thirsty Camel.* Apparently, they all chimed in about how pretty I was and said they'd never seen him so happy. Ah, yes, nothing says *no pressure* like a bar-room endorsement from the good old boys down at the Camel.

When his last phone call *assaulted* my phone a few days later (after a whole week of official dating) my internal voice shouted "Fuck off!", but I said it out loud as well. I didn't answer. Instead, I took out the *breakup text* I had composed on a Post-it the night before, polished it up, dropped it in a text bubble and hit send.

It was kind.

It was caring.

It was as honest as I could be.

BOOM. Off it went.

And then, of course, the wait. How bad was this going to get? Was he going to throw some bitchy insult my way? Or worse?

Then—*Ping!*—his reply came in. I hesitated. Took a deep breath. Braced for the storm.

His message? "Goodbye. I knew it."

A minute later, as expected, he followed up with a passive-aggressive insult (I'll let your imagination run wild with that one). Yep, he'd seen it coming. Maybe even *manifested* it. Honestly, even across our two dates, his insecurities kept bubbling up. I think, deep down, he always knew this was going to happen.

And he was right. Jacob... Out!

Here's a little tidbit of wisdom for anyone thinking, *"Why didn't you just tell him where he was slipping up? Why not ask him to back off, give you some breathing room, and stop being so needy?"*

Well, here's the trick—something I've learned from a few dating experts I follow—if you *do* tell them, sure, they might adjust their behavior... but only temporarily. Just long enough to gain your trust. And then? They revert. Fall right back into the patterns that have been embedded in them—likely since childhood, or from some deep, unresolved trauma.

We all carry some sort of trauma or trigger we're working through. That's just part of being human. But here's the thing: *that's his work to do, not mine.* I'm not here to save men from themselves.

As someone who's always been fascinated by human behavior and the wild, wonderful complexity of the human condition, I still find myself wondering (along with the anthropologists and armchair psychologists): *How do male/female/non-binary relationships ever last?* Seriously.

If you're one of the lucky ones who truly finds *the One*, then great—go you. But for the rest of us? It's a struggle. We date. We marry. We divorce. And then sometimes we do it all over again—maybe more than twice. Even when we're past the age, the urge, or the *capability* of procreating, something in our DNA, in our primal Neanderthal wiring, keeps us searching. Sniffing out connection. Craving a mate.

I suppose it comes down to the fact that we're social animals. We thrive on companionship. We want to know—deep down—that someone loves us, someone *chooses* us (besides our kids or our moms).

Of course, I'm sure some of you out there might want to debate that. And honestly? I welcome it.

Oddly enough, this entry comes after a few glasses... okay, *a lot* of glasses of wine and some blues music to really help me sink into the mood I'm in. And, surprisingly, I'm kind of amazed at how well I type under the influence.

Naturally, in this state, you start thinking a little deeper about life. It's like smoking a joint (haven't done that in ages) where everything suddenly feels profound, like, *"Wow... this is the meaning of life."* LOL. But of course, it's not *really*. Still, the thoughts came, and I figured I'd share a few revelations—if they even count as that.

I started wondering: *Is this what I envisioned my life to be? Is this how I thought it would unfold?* Honestly, I don't think I ever really painted a clear picture. When I was 20... 30... even into my 40s, I don't remember imagining scenarios. I was just living—taking life one day, one week, maybe a month at a time. No big agenda, just trying to be happy in the moment.

And here I am now, at 69, asking myself: *Did I do it right? What really matters? Would I have made different choices?*

The truth? Yeah, probably. But also... everything I've experienced—every high, low, misstep, and triumph—has shaped me. And you know what? *I like myself.* I like who I've become.

That said, am I where I thought I'd be? Not exactly. But this is my reality. This is where I've landed. I've lived a *lot* of life. Good, bad, and plenty of "What the hell was I thinking?" moments. But I've come to terms with who I am. I know my values. And I'm honestly happy with how I'm "turning out." LOL.

In the end, the fluff doesn't matter—the material stuff, the missteps, even some of the regrets. I have a beautiful family. I have friends who value me, and I them. I've done my best, in every situation. I have integrity. I own my shit. And I've survived *a lot.*

And for that, I'm proud. Proud of how I've lived—*generally speaking.*

But, after all is said and done, I am—somewhat—alone. Not lonely, really... but alone in not having someone to share the *intimate* parts of life with. The day-to-day stuff. The good days, the bad ones. Someone to talk to at the end of it all. Someone to wrap me in a hug and say, "I'm here for you—every step of the way."

Sure, you get *pieces* of that from friends and family. But it's the *intimate* moments—the ones where you're vulnerable, unguarded, raw—that you miss. That you *need.* And that... that is what I'm striving for.

Because at our core, we're all wired for *connection.* Deep connection. The kind that reaches into your gut and stays there. That soul-touching, "See me and love me anyway" kind of bond. That's what we crave.

So, on this wild journey—through horrendous dating sites and constant wondering if I'll *ever* meet someone who adds *that* kind of magic to my life again (if anyone ever really did), I still hold onto the hope that it's possible. That someone is out there.

That said, I *am* grateful. Truly. For everything I've had, the beauty I've seen, and the joy I've felt—pure, exuberant joy. And if I were to die tomorrow, I could say my life was full. *Very* full.

I believe I've experienced more than most. I've done things that many wouldn't even imagine doing. And in that sense, I've been lucky. To still be alive? Honestly, that might be a miracle in itself.

The few things I've shared with close friends about my life are usually met with: *"Wow! You should write a book."*

(Which, as you can see, I *am.*)

Because yeah—I've lived an interesting life.

But I'm not done yet.

Sure, I'm 69 (and yes, the mind *does* wander to the perverse with that particular number), but I plan on living a few more decades. That is, in fact, one of my life goals. So, here's to more adventures—and a few more juicy chapters—before I decide to type "*The End*."

# Chapter 15

As before, the time-space continuum has fast-forwarded; about a month has passed since I last updated this book. Dating, had been reduced to the sad, slow drip of a leaky tap with a worn-out washer. My two dating apps were reduced to flushing out the leftover debris stuck deep inside the plumbing of the virtual world—men who apparently forgot how to brush their hair, smile, or put on a clean shirt. The *basics*, really.

Gone were the days of hopeful fish pics (still ridiculous, but at least they were outdoors). Now? We've descended into guys lying shirtless on unmade beds, hoping to seduce. This is what was bubbling up from the depths of the abyss.

Interestingly, a Facebook group I follow—"Burned Haystack Dating Method"—offers some solid insight. The whole idea is burn down all the hay (aka the crap), and what's left is the *needle*. Their posts are full of fascinating and brutally honest information about how to decode the red flags, rhetorical patterns and subtext in dating profiles. Honestly? Most enlightening. Actually, a method you can use in your everyday life to suss out what people are *really* saying to you. If so inclined, it's worth a Facebook search into this group - 215K strong. Jennie Young is the creator and owner and has her PhD in rhetoric and discourse studies, and in this case, acknowledging and deciphering the "rhetorical patterns" that present themselves in the dating world. Valuable stuff.

Anyway, Jennie, once ran a survey asking women whether they were drawn to or repelled by shirtless, overly sexual profile pictures.

The result? A resounding 99% of responses fell into the categories of: "No thanks," "Ick," and every variation of the vomiting emoji.

Only 1% were cool with it.

If only men *knew*. How do we make them stop?

We don't. We just swipe left.

But as my focus, interest and energy moved further and further away from the dating apps, and into the figurative embrace of my gal pals, I did feel a bit of loneliness lurking quietly in the shadows.

Which is why I had adopted a kitty.

I wanted another heartbeat in the room. Someone who would be happy to see me at the end of a workday.

And to that end, of my sweet, adorable, playful, mischievous, stubborn, relentless, *deaf* kitty cat who had punctured, scratched, toppled, and maneuvered into every nook and cranny in my place, I had come to a conclusion: It was a love/hate relationship.

So adorable, sweeter than caramel on a hot chocolate sundae when she was sleeping, but when she was awake, it was a game of psychological warfare. She tested my patience constantly.

As much as I loved her (and all animals for that matter), she brought out anger in me that I didn't know I had (ok... well, maybe I knew). If someone had snapped a photo of me, with spray bottle in hand, red faced, fire shooting from my eyes and evil words spewing from my mouth, you'd swear the devil him/herself had been released. Terrifying.

But why (Why?!) would she jump on my table 6 times in five minutes just to hear the words, "Get the fuck off of there!" Was she so desperate for attention that anything would suffice?

(As a side note, so you don't think I'm a complete monster, I felt terrible after and always followed up with kind words and a kiss).

I did work from home, but my office was a No Cat Zone. Not because I was heartless, but because she found trouble within minutes, knocking stuff over, biting cords, papers avalanching to the floor, then glaring at me like I was the problem. The distraction and chaos were too much. I truly needed to focus.

Cuddle time? That happened in the morning for about five minutes on the couch, with a little kneading, drooling and purring (on her part). She announced she was done by sinking her sharp teeth into my hand, then off she would go. She had plans, missions and an agenda.

If a door opened, she raced in so fast you'd think her life depended on it. My bedroom and my office were her ultimate goals. If she got past the door frames (think goal posts), she'd hide so I couldn't grab her. This led to the ever popular find-a-toy-that-rattles and throw it out of the room. Thankfully, she never caught on to my ruse and always fired off to chase it. Door closed. I win.

Of course, in her defense, she was only being a cat, but my later attempts to cuddle only turned to bites and physical attacks and my furniture got more and more shredded during her *zoomies* episodes. It started to look like a war zone/obstacle course. Blankets on all my furniture, tin foil cookie sheets on the tables and around my plants, and spiked mats forming the do-not-cross borders. It wasn't the home I imagined. No peaceful retreat. My calm oasis had become a battleground and I was becoming increasingly miserable. And completely stressed.

We weren't a good match and I couldn't keep trying.

So, the difficult decision was made to call the owner, Angela, of the little pig farm from whence she came. I gave a somewhat made up but plausible excuse *that I had been promoted to client relationship manager and would have to travel to our Calgary office on a somewhat regular basis. I had no one to watch her while I was gone, so I had to make the heartbreaking decision to rehome her.*

Angela, who was kind and understanding, came by to rescue my *sweet* feline two days later.

Still, it was a sad day. Sadder than I thought it might be. I was expecting more of a sense of relief but it was overshadowed by my heartbreak. Sure, I got my home back, but I also had to let go of little Bella.

I cried—a lot, especially that night after she left. I was riddled with guilt and sadness and an apartment that was echoing with silence. Her soul still felt present, but she was gone. Her sweet, adorable, puffy cheeks, pink nose, purry little soul had left.

And, again, I cried the next day.

But there is a joyful part to this story.

She hadn't been rehomed with strangers. She had been returned to her mom and siblings, who still resided at the quirky little farm just outside the city limits.

It was a magical little spot called *Pigtopia* and there, along with Angela and her husband, was an entire staff (and family members) that ran this tiny operation where the public could come out and pet the piggies–and maybe adopt them. (Not sure.) But she also had cats. Lots of cats. Twenty-six to be exact!

Angela loved them all. This was her life. All lovingly looked after and cared for. And her obvious commitment had been reinforced both times I met up with her. Stocky, hearty, joyful and always sporting a unique look with a pink knitted pig hat, bomber jacket and rubber boats. Yep, she was all in!

The next day, I sent off a text to *Ms. Piggy* to check on my little Bella Boo (which I affectionately called her on occasion) and she comforted me by telling me that Bella and her mom had spent the night together quite happily. Turns out, I wasn't a monster. Just a person who made a difficult decision.

A few months passed, and I rarely thought of Kitty, though her photos remained on my phone. I tried not to look at them as I scrolled past while looking for something else, and my heart would ache just a little. She was a holy terror but she was my holy terror.

# Chapter 16

My focus had shifted once again. Work had taken center stage, and dating apps got nothing more than a casual glance now and then. They didn't feel important anymore. Still part of my agenda, but I was evolving.

Over the next few months, *work* took on a whole new aggravation of its own. My boss was all over the map, one day kind and understanding, the next, ripping a strip off me over something that had nothing to do with me. His tone was condescending, and the same tired grievances began playing on repeat like a broken record.

I had to train myself to mentally block out his rants. They were upsetting, often robbing me of sleep. On a few occasions, I lectured him back demanding respect and expressing my lack of appreciation for his attitude and arrogance. But it was short lived.

As the weeks blurred together, I decided I needed out. For the sake of my sanity and self-worth, I started browsing *job* sites instead of dating sites—plotting my escape.

And then, before I could make a move, one of the employees quit, for personal health reasons. And a few days later, I got hit with the news: I was being laid off. The reason? He couldn't afford me.

Honestly, I could barely muster a reaction.

I'd been down this road so many times, even my PTSD didn't flare up like it used to. I was *done* with him—done with his erratic behavior and god-awful management skills. In some twisted way, it felt like a blessing.

The downside? He didn't pay me my final cheque, and the measly two-week severance he offered? Still in limbo.

And to top it all off, he never issued a tax slip despite months of me asking (and being met with crickets). So, I had to get my accountant to create one based on pay stubs I *never actually saw. Not that I didn't request them.* He always had an excuse such as "QuickBooks isn't working right now".

I submitted a complaint to the government and filed for EI. Because, thankfully, *laid off* meant I could at least claim something. Or so I thought...

Work...dating. Work...dating. Not sure which was worse at that point.

However...

Mid-May we were back to dating. I'm scrolling and swiping left with a level of enthusiasm hovering around 2%, one eye barely open, when—*bam*—one fetching guy catches my attention.

I stop.

Stare.

I raise an eyebrow.

Twist my lips in that skeptical-but-intrigued way.

I read his profile while simultaneously scanning the other hot photos he submitted. Then I do a double take. Profile again. Photos again. Still no red flags.

Using my one trained (and still-open) eye, I gave him the full once-over. He passed the test. So, with a flicker of renewed excitement, I swiped right and tapped the little heart icon like it meant something again.

And that's when life got interesting.

Light shone down upon me from above.

Repressed hope slowly floated back to the surface.

A few hours later—*ding, ding, ding*—he swiped right too. We were a match! Darryl was my new *Next*.

From there, the texts started flowing—back and forth, light and easy, full of curiosity, comfort, and trust. Once I decided he was sincere, legit, and (yes) *still handsome*, I gave him my phone number.

We jumped ship from Facebook's awkward little chat box and dove into full-blown texting, complete with photo sharing, emojis, and all the things we actually *felt* like saying.

Thankfully, he wasn't one of those endless-text guys. Within days, we had a date set.

No slow-burn nonsense. No ghosting games. Just... genuine interest.

So, fast-forward—without boring you with minute-by-minute recaps—our first date was seven hours long: hiking through the river valley, followed by dinner.

The second date? Six hours of pool, food, and deep conversation—trading stories, uncovering all these weird and wonderful things we had in common. Of course, the flirt factor dialed up, too.

And then... date three.

*The infamous one.*

Dinner at my place. More flirtatious banter.

And yes, the *sleepover.*

Dare I say it? It was amazing!

The next morning, after that amazing night (sorry, not sorry), he had to head out of town—about three hours away—for a big construction job. He'd likely be gone for a week, maybe a bit more.

We texted every few days, but I missed him since a small connection had been established.

As the week dragged on, three entire days passed where I didn't hear a single word from him. Nothing. Nada. Crickets.

And just like that, I fell into my usual spiral of doom.

My mind became a horror show of worst-case scenarios:

"It's over."

"I scared him off."

"I'll never see him again."

Cue obsessive Googling:

*What does it mean if he doesn't text for 3 days?*

*Should I text first or play hard to get?*

*Signs he's ghosting you.*

*Has he moved on?*

Yes, I went there. I always do. I'm an anxious dater.

Eventually, I caved. I texted him casually. At least I tried to sound casual.

"Hey D, how's the project going?"

And just like that, my little tormented brain started to calm. He replied. Quickly. Kindly. Definitely still interested.

And then? The flirting was back. Some hot, playful, delightful banter followed. Not all at once, but throughout the day. It was fun and all that was needed.

A little spark to quiet the internal chaos. I could finally breathe again.

The next week passed quickly, and Darryl was now back in town. We locked in our fourth date. One I had deemed *pivotal* in the grand scheme of *us*.

Why? Well, we'd already crossed the consummation threshold on our last encounter, and I needed to know this wasn't just about my (clearly irresistible) body. I needed affirmation. Reassurance.

And you know what? It was another *great* night.

We played pool—something we both loved and, frankly, were damn good at. I even kicked his ass a few times, much to my own delight. After sinking a few balls (and a few drinks), we grabbed a bite, flirted shamelessly, and soaked in each other's company. Eventually, I invited him back to my place to continue the reunion—two weeks apart had secured a little after-hours celebration.

Back home, we played crib, we chatted, and (as was becoming our pattern), things turned towards another intimate encounter. No disappointment there. Again.

But as the post-passion dissipated, he was *out like a light.*

Men have this incredible ability to pass out mid-breath, anywhere, anytime, especially after some action. Meanwhile, I did the usual—removed my makeup, brushed my teeth, mentally replayed every moment—and tried to settle next to a man I wasn't yet comfortable sleeping beside. Because yeah, I don't just fall asleep next to a virtual stranger, no matter how many dates have passed. That takes time.

Morning came early—*too* early. Darryl, up with the birds, while I attempted to cling to my much needed beauty sleep. As he got ready to leave, and after a few sleepy mutters between us, it happened.

He said:

"What was that, sweetie?"

*Sweetie.* My brain latched onto it like a lifeline.

*Had we shifted? Leveled up? Did this mean something?*

In my anxious, romantic, overthinking-female brain...I really wanted to believe that.

Now, I had already established that Darryl wasn't much of a texter—days could go by without a single word—but that didn't stop the self-doubt from creeping in. I still wrestled with those relentless negative thoughts: *"It's over," "He's lost interest," "If he really liked me, wouldn't he text every day?"* Anxiety brain is a special kind of hell.

But then came the kicker. A big one. A stab to the heart and a punch to the gut. I wasn't prepared for this one.

A now *ex* friend of mine (not as a result from this incident), sent me a text, along with a screenshot of a face I knew only too well.

Her message:

"Before I swipe right on this guy... isn't this the one you've been dating?"

Flattened.

Speechless.

Shocked.

I sat there, frozen with that sickening *Zing* moment rushing through my body – similar to when you catch your man kissing someone else. That split second when your heart hits the floor and your brain scrambles to catch up. Yeah. That.

What followed was a whole lot of, "Fuck! Fuck, fuck, fuuuuck," spewing from my lips as I registered the shock. Once I caught my breath and a new set of wheels started to spin in my mind, my friend and I hatched what I'll call a *sinister* plan (though really, it was just a clever bit of recon).

She wasn't interested in dating him—*and even if she had been,* she'd never go against a sista. Girl code, solid. Instead, she agreed to swipe right and string him along just enough to expose his *game.*

"Operation Honeytrap Hotline" was launched. She kept me updated with screenshots of their convo. To his credit (or maybe discredit?), he stuck to his story. No blatant lies. When asked if he'd had any dating luck, he admitted he'd met someone "compatible"—presumably me. But still, he was out there. Fishing. Playing the field. And clearly *not* off the market.

That changed everything.

We hadn't had the *exclusive* talk, so technically he wasn't breaking any rules. But it still hurt. And more than that, it shifted something deep inside me. I started emotionally pulling back, and re-evaluating whether I wanted to continue investing in a man who wasn't putting his focus solely on *me.* Or was it just the dread of starting over again?

And then came another gut punch.

He told my friend he was "seeing about four women"—some for hiking, some with chemistry—and, apparently, he was sleeping with *none* of them. Except... he was sleeping with *me.* So... lie.

He said he was dating "with no expectations and no pressure."

Translation: *I'm a player. I like attention. Don't catch feelings.*

At that point, I didn't know what to believe.

And I certainly didn't know how I could enjoy any future time with him without a mental picture of me stabbing him in my head... or maybe just one well-placed kick to his (otherwise perfect) balls. Sorry not sorry.

I deserved more.

More honesty. More respect. More reciprocity.

So, I gathered up all the self-worth, dignity, and inner power I could muster, and I wrote him a final message. Maybe it was more for *me*—a way to stop the obsessive thoughts bouncing around in my head—but either way, it needed to be said.

My *Dear John* text read:

*"Hey Darryl. So can't do Monday. I rather doubt any night. I think we're on different pages. I know you're seeing other women, which is fine since we're not exclusive. But since you didn't let me know, you put my health at risk (assuming you're having unprotected sex with them as well). I respect myself too much to continue seeing you since I feel open communication and trust is needed.*

*I had fun with you but we want different things. I need more than sex! You asked me once why I'm still single... I think you answered your own question.*

*BTW, my close friend, who you chatted with, was kind enough to screenshot all of your conversations. It's a very small world, Darryl, and I have a LOT of single friends. Take care.*

*I know you probably don't give a shit anyway."*

I hit send with only a tiny twinge of sadness – because he *did seem* to be a pretty nice guy underneath it all. I never expected a reply (takes balls and class to do that) and to no surprise, I never received one. So, onto the next.

*As a side note (and good to know if you're ever traveling down the dark road of online dating), there are various groups on social media that post "dangerous and shady characters," or ones with too many red flags, on dating sites. It's basically women looking after women and their safety. Lots of repeat offenders. Do a name search, and up they pop! Apparently, good old Darryl has been an ongoing headliner.*

# Chapter 17

Dating out; back to work! Vicious circle!

Finding a job and fighting with my ex-employer continued.

I was still knee-deep in the trenches, fighting tooth and nail for my severance from my ex-boss—let's call him *Richard (or perhaps the shorter version, Dick)* to protect his *precious anonymity.*

Along with that, I needed one *very* important piece of paper: the infamous ROE—Record of Employment—which, for those blessedly unaware, is the golden ticket required to actually apply for unemployment income in this governmental circus we call a system.

After what felt like a dozen gracious (and then not-so-gracious) attempts to extract said severance and ROE from Richard, I finally brought in the big guns.

Yep. I called in the *government agents. Cue Mission Impossible music.*

So now, on top of dating stress, ghosting anxiety, and the usual spiral of emotional free-falls, I had a full-blown employment conflict to add to the list.

Because why not? When it rains, it *absolutely fucking pours.*

**Author's note: Due to legal implications and possible repercussions at a later date, this chapter has been edited to protect the innocent. The fun, spicy details have been deleted.*

A month had passed, and still no ROE. Which meant *still* no income from Employment Insurance. Not a dime. And as for the severance money? Nowhere in sight. Official complaints had been filed and submitted, so I was left at the mercy of overworked government agencies, buried under paper piles and red tape.

Apparently, the severance claim could take up to four months just to be *looked at*, and the EI complaint? Probably sitting on a desk with a sticky note that says "someday." You know how that goes.

At this point, I was seriously considering bringing in a lawyer—or at the very least, the threat of one. Richard, of course, was doing what he did best: playing ostrich. Head buried deep in the sand, pretending that if *he* couldn't see me, then *I* didn't exist. Classic.

But this time, I had a plan. I drafted one last text. Calm, clear... and laced with just enough legal venom to shake him out of his black hole. I included a little excerpt I found online that spelled things out quite nicely:

*"Failure to submit a Record of Employment may result in a $2,000 fine or six months in jail."*

Short, sweet, and hopefully enough to make him picture orange jumpsuits, shared toilets and "Big Tats" in the corner who likes the young ones. And let's not forget—the ROE was just the beginning.

But honestly? At this point, it wasn't even about the money anymore. It was about *justice*. About the audacity of someone thinking they could treat people like shit, then disappear into the fog. My anger and frustration were no longer a simmer—it was a damn boil. It followed me into my dreams and greeted me every morning the second I opened my eyes.

And to top it all off? Job hunting was going nowhere. And I could feel it—*desperation was starting to creep in.*

I launched the next strike via text—firm, clear, and loaded with legal receipts. I attached a screenshot from the government website, complete with bolded penalties: *"$2,000 fine or six months in jail for failure to submit an ROE."* Then I followed it up with a not-so-sweet message, "If I don't receive the correct ROE by the end of the week, I'll be proceeding with legal action."

The days of the polite, blonde, people-pleasing version of me? Over. She was dead. Buried. Cremated. Scattered at sea.

One hour later, my phone dinged. An email. From Richard.

*Subject: ROE*

*"Please find attached. All the best, Richard."*

Oh, so *now* he wants to play Mr. Professional.

I was out running errands, Starbucks in hand, but the second I saw that email, I swerved into the nearest parking lot stall like it was a pit stop at the Indy 500. *This was it.*

Quick review.

Slower review.

Analytical review.

*Eagle-eyed forensic accountant review.*

And that's when I felt the fury creep up my spine like a snake about to strike.

The hours? Wrong.

The total earnings? *Wrong.*

The reason for leaving? WRONG.

Excuse me? *Dismissed?!* I wasn't dismissed–I was laid the fuck off. Where'd he pull that from?

My jaw clenched. I felt my muscles tense up like I was about to arm-wrestle a bear. This wasn't over.

Overwhelmed, and honestly just *exhausted*, I headed home and flopped down in front of my computer for a more detailed inspection of the now infamous ROE. I knew it wasn't right, but I needed to be 100% sure. And yup—confirmed. It was garbage.

So, I dialed up Service Canada for the *second* time that day, brought them up to speed, and added this latest twist to my already overstuffed complaint file. They walked me through the next steps and promised to escalate it further. I ended the call and... saw a missed call from Richard.

Oh? Look who found a phone.

I took a deep breath, pulled myself together, and called him back. He answered, a little too quickly, with a nervous, "Hey, how are you?"

I paused, let the silence hang for a second or two, and said—calm, cool, and absolutely seething, "Not happy."

And from there? I unleashed.

Words flew out of me like angry bees from a poked hive— firm, fast, and impossible to swat away. He tried to fumble out a few lame excuses, but I wasn't having any of it. I kept my tone even and steady, channelling pure Judge Judy.

To his credit—or maybe just in self-preservation—he eventually *apologized*. He admitted his silence had made things worse and confessed that he'd handled the whole situation poorly. No kidding.

I calmly reiterated the facts (like the spreadsheet warrior I was):

- The ROE must reflect the correct hours and wages, per the email I sent.
- My severance must be paid out by the end of the week.
- No more games. No more silence. Just do your job.

ROEs cost nothing to file. And my measly severance wasn't going to sink the ship. This wasn't about money anymore—it was about principle. And I was done playing nice.

A month or two had passed, and summer was winding down... but *guess what hadn't shown up yet*?

Yup. Still no ROE. Still no severance. Still no decency from the guy I once referred to as my boss.

By now, my *legal agent*—the title I was sworn to use, like I'd just hired a hitman from the employment section of the CIA—had stepped up our game plan. We were going full throttle into legal warfare.

It was time to sue.

At this point, the only explanation for his continued ghosting—after the Demand Letter, the complaints, the threats, the texts, the calls, the mild-to-moderate cursing—was that he was *desperately* trying to stay under the radar.

We were moving forward with the civic claim, ready to drag this man into the uncomfortable spotlight of justice. He'd have 20 days to cough up a hefty wad of cash—more than just my severance—thanks to legal fees, damages, and the mental toll of turning me into a professional complainer who knew Service Canada's hold music by heart.

All this, because he couldn't be bothered to submit a simple form and write a basic cheque. But instead, it was now about to cost him big—*liens on property vibes*, at the very least.

And if he so much as *dared* show up in court with another whiny excuse, I would have to exercise extreme restraint not to throw a stapler at him.

Because I was no longer the sweet, compliant girl from my previous life —the people-pleaser with a plastered smile and a bruised backbone. That girl had left the building.

This guy didn't just delay paperwork. He restructured my entire life. My finances, my mental health and my physical health. I even sold family heirlooms and my gold jewelry to make ends meet. Retribution was in order!

# Chapter 18

Setting business aside and taking a breather from the legal turmoil, I ventured out to visit a very old friend of mine for some escapism and a lovely dinner.

The quick backstory on this old bud of mine, Sam, is someone I've known since the late 80's, attended his many epic house parties, and even became intimate for a short while. Over the last few years, both his parents succumbed to Alzheimer's and Sam had essentially given up his life to care for them. They both passed within a year of each other and Sam, although grieving, was able to resume his slightly fractured life. Sad of course but they were blessed with nine decades of life, love and adventures.

So, I went over to catch up, and, in some ways, console him over the recent loss of his parents. It was bittersweet of course, both freeing and heart-breaking.

With each of us having plenty to catch up on and lifetimes of chaos to unpack, Sam and I shared stories over dinner and dessert like two old souls trading scars. The night was Canadian tropical—one of those late-summer evenings where the heat just hangs in the air like a weighted blanket. Not to waste our short summers, we ventured outside, with wine in hand, to soak in the warm dusk and the slow, magenta sunset.

Then, to make things a *bit* more interesting (because clearly our lives weren't already spicy enough), Sam pulled out his vape pipe—pre-loaded with some high-quality herb. I hadn't really smoked in years. My days of giving into Mary Jane were long past, and now I stuck to the occasional puff here and there, just to take the edge off.

So, I said, *"Sure, one little puff."*

Yeah. *Big mistake.*

Apparently, vapes are nothing like the casual, mouth-kiss of a joint. This devious little machine delivered what felt like the entire contents of a forest fire into my lungs, and I watched in horror as I exhaled a giant, swirling cloud like I was auditioning to be the next Puff the Magic Dragon.

Within *seconds*, I knew I was toast. My entire sense of self started to drift into the night sky like a helium balloon on a windy day. And just like that, I was floating—completely detached from my body and grasping desperately at some invisible tether to reality.

What followed was three hours of the strangest conversation I will never remember. I'd ask a question—just to prove I could still function—and by the time Sam was two sentences into his response, I'd already forgotten what I asked. My brain was like a screen door in a hurricane.

I kept telling myself, *"Never again. I'd rather be drunk and devouring nachos than be a cloud of atoms and molecules in existential limbo."*

Finally, around midnight, I started feeling semi-human again. I could do basic math. I could remember my middle name. And I began the mental gymnastics of figuring out if I could drive home—or if I'd be spending the night spooning a throw pillow on Sam's couch.

I chose to risk the drive. However, I increased my water intake and did a few on the spot jumping jacks to get my blood recirculating. I then carefully plotted my escape via back roads—no freeways, no big intersections, just me, some empty streets, and a prayer.

The good news? I made it.

The bad news? I *almost* made it.

I pulled up to my building, swiped the key fob, celebrated my safe landing... and then, in one bad turn taken one thousand times before, I clipped the side of my car along a yellow utility pipe in the underground garage.

Not a dent. Just a huge, ugly, mocking yellow stripe from bumper to door. Like the universe tagging me with a big ol', "Nice try, stoner."

The next day, with a little WD-40, a sponge, and the strength of a thousand regrets, I buffed that memory out too.

Verdict: I'm sticking with wine.

Smoking too much weed aside, I was *very* glad I wasn't high one particular evening when I finally wandered off to bed around 1:00 a.m. (yes, I'm a night owl). I'd barely drifted off when I was jolted awake by a weird, mechanical buzzing sound coming from the bathroom. Half-asleep and mildly freaked out, I slowly got up and opened the door—only to discover that my electric toothbrush had gone *full Chucky* on me.

There it was, standing upright on its little charging base, *vibrating like it had a personal vendetta*. I'd had this toothbrush for a solid year—reliable, loyal, well-behaved. But tonight? It was clearly possessed. Buzzing, rattling, shaking—like it had unfinished business with my molars.

Trying to stay calm, I flipped on the light, unplugged it, and separated the brush head from the handle. I figured that would shut it up. Problem solved, right?

Wrong.

Five minutes later—*Bzzzzzzz*—off it went *again*, unprompted and undead.

At this point, I was less spooked and more pissed off. I stomped back in like an avenging dental hygienist, ripped the brush head off again, and started furiously stabbing at the rubber-covered power button with a pair of scissors. But no—this toothbrush was not done. It buzzed louder, as if mocking me. It was like trying to kill Godzilla with a butter knife.

Finally, it sputtered out a few half-hearted vibrations and seemed to die.

I exhaled. I tucked myself back in.

And *then*—yes, you guessed it—*Round Three*.

This time, I was *done* playing nice. I stormed back in like I was in *The Conjuring*, holy water and imaginary crucifix in hand. I went full exorcist on this evil little bastard. The toothbrush was no longer an appliance—it was an enemy. I cracked open the exterior, gouged out the tiny demonic motherboard inside, and with fury in my eyes and dramatic flair, I flung its remains out into the rainy night like a one-woman ghostbuster.

"Die, you bastard!" I screamed internally.

Don't. Mess. With. Sharon. Demon killed!

The next morning, with a slight case of exorcism fatigue, I logged into Amazon and ordered a new one. In a nice passive pink.

Because if I'm going to fight off haunted appliances, I might as well do it in style.

Life is weird.

Anyway, this is the *perfect segue* into my next creepy-but-comical experience. Not quite trauma-level, but definitely something that made me go, "Of course this would happen to me."

One early and very rainy Wednesday morning, I dragged myself to a Senior Housing information session. I was doing my due diligence, looking into possible subsidized rentals—because let's face it, my financial situation wasn't exactly thriving, and I needed to start coming up with viable options.

As I arrived, one thing was *very* clear: I was the baby of the bunch. The crowd was a sea of white hair (if there was any left), canes, walkers, and sweet little slippers that probably hadn't left the front door in weeks. But hey, even if I felt a bit out of place, my near-future needs aligned with theirs. So, I sat down, ready to listen.

What I *wasn't* ready for, was the random flirtation ambush.

As we were settling into our rusty fold-out chairs, a man—if we can call him that—shuffled his way right into the vacant seat beside me. I pegged him at about 5 foot 2 inches, which meant that, unfortunately, his head was basically at *boob level* with me. And that's precisely where his eyes seemed to land... and linger, as he nestled into his chair.

I noticed him scanning me like I was a 30%-off rotisserie chicken at the grocery store. Top to bottom. Real slow. Like he was debating whether to make a move or just say grace and tuck in a napkin.

My friend, sitting on the other side of me, *totally* noticed and nearly lost it. I could see her shoulders bouncing from suppressed laughter, and I was trying to contain both my giggles and my internal *gag reflex.* I clutched my brochures to my chest like a makeshift chastity guard, stared straight ahead, and tried to focus on the PowerPoint presentation about senior rent caps and walk in bathtubs.

But it was hard to ignore the unsettling energy radiating from the *pocket-sized hobbit* next to me.

Anyway, lesson learned: even senior housing meetings come with surprise encounters. At least I walked out with some housing brochures *and* a reminder that creepy doesn't retire—it just shows up late and finds the one last seat next to you.

# Chapter 19

As hard as it is to meet *quality* men, I found out it's equally hard—if not harder—to meet quality women. And I say that as someone who genuinely enjoys female friendships and was fully invested in having a solid circle.

During my wildly difficult year of 2024, overflowing as it was with financial chaos, escalating back pain, a never-ending job search, diabolical kittens, and the stress of an ongoing court case, I was hit with yet another lovely surprise: I lost seven friends. All in one fell swoop. *Poof.* Gone.

Now, this is a bit of a long story, but here's the truncated version. I belong to a huge women's community via Facebook—about 20,000 members strong. From that, smaller subgroups had branched off: golf lovers, single moms, book clubs, DYI-ers, wine enthusiasts... you name it. As noted earlier, I had created the group *Singles Mingles*. The original vision was to band together and locate where all the elusive *quality* men were hiding. Kind of like a hot guy scavenger hunt.

But as with most things, the plan evolved. After a few months, it became less about man-hunting and more about just getting out to have fun. Sharing war stories and living a little as the fierce women that we were.

The group gathered about 200 members, but—as is the case with most online communities—only about 1% actually showed up to anything. That 1%? My core group of seven. My ride-or-die sisters. My weekend crew.

Over the course of a year and many, many months, I spent a ton of time with these women. We hit bars, checked out restaurants, went to local events, and shared a lot of laughs (and wine). These were the people I vented to about my ex-boss, who sat beside me when my back was in spasm, who knew about the frustrating depths of my job hunt. And, in my defense, I only focused about 5 – 10 minutes, tops, on these subjects because someone asked.

They were my people... or so I thought.

During the late summer, one of the ladies (and I'm being generous using the term "lady") decided to start a new group with some clichéd name. The group got posted on our community site, and—like everyone else—I submitted a request to join. The usual protocol.

*As I patiently waited for my anticipated "Welcome. You're in" prompt from the group leader, I received a slap in the face instead.* I got *declined.* Rejected. Dismissed. By the very people I had wined, dined, and danced with for over a year.

Stunned, I reached out with a simple, fair question: *Why?*

The leader (a self-proclaimed title, I might add – I just call her bitch) responded that they'd be doing "more expensive things" and that I probably wouldn't fit in. That's right—apparently my bank balance wasn't up to their high-brow lunch standards. Shock turned quickly to rage. I fired back with a direct, assertive response: "How dare you judge and discriminate against me based on my financial situation."

I was hurt. Genuinely wounded. I'd been open with them. Shared my real struggles. Laughed. Cried. Paid for Ubers and dinners when others didn't. And this was the thanks?

Then came the kicker—a seven-paragraph text from the ringleader herself, dripping with arrogance and passive-aggressive venom. She outlined, in obsessive detail, every conversation, every complaint, every moment of my so-called "drama." Apparently, she'd been taking notes like she was building a case against me in Small Claims Court. Who *does* that? Who catalogs someone else's pain? The cherry on top? She flat-out said, *"I do not like you, and we are not friends."*

Angered but not willing to sink to her level, I gave myself a day to respond. Drafted it. Slept on it. Refined it. And took the high road, because I *am* better than that. Better than her.

Here's what I sent:

*"Yah, I could definitely argue on many of your points, and most of what you've said is just your perspective. I paid for a lot of things—including more than my share of Ubers. But considering your obvious dislike for me, it's not worth my energy or time to defend myself. Nor should I have to.*

*But I must say—I'm quite flattered that you took such detailed notes on my life."*

Of course, in the days that followed, I kept thinking of all the zingers I *should* have said (don't we all?). Gems like:

- *"Oh no—you don't like me? Give me a moment to recover*

*from the tragedy."*

- *"Careful, Bonnie, lest you suffer vertigo from the dizzying heights of your moral ground."*
- And my personal fav: *"Sweetie, if you don't like me, it's probably because I didn't want you to."*

But the truth is, that whole group of *friends* vanished in a puff of righteous smoke. Not a single one reached out to check on me. Well... except for a few hitting *Like* on a Facebook post. So yeah—fuck them all.

Thankfully, I *do* have real friends. The kind who lift me up when I'm down, who don't count how many times I vent, who know that life gets messy and that true connection doesn't come with terms and conditions.

Those are the keepers.

As for the rest?

**NEXT.**

To summarize this dark part of my story (the Ying and the Yang) 2024 was one of the most difficult years of my life as this list of events, touched on above, clearly shows:

1. Financial struggles, partly due to an ex-employer that

wouldn't provide proper documents, severance or, as the battle continued, acknowledgement of a civil claim or additional documents that followed.

2. Unable to claim and receive Employment Insurance – so no income coming in.
3. A physical disability that delivers steady pain or continual discomfort (it hurts just to sit here and type).
4. Losing a group of friends – who perhaps were never real friends
5. Trying to find suitable employment (although I did find a part-time job via a temp agency, but the assignment was almost an hour drive, and contributed to my back pain).
6. Receiving notice of a rental increase of $200, creating even more urgency to move and find an apartment I could actually afford.
7. Hitting dead ends in almost all areas when trying to seek assistance and additional senior benefits from the government;
8. Continued to have great difficulty finding decent apartments with vacancies.

It's been stressful. Depressing, exhausting, and at times, downright hopeless, waiting for something truly great to come my way.

Sure, I've had joyful moments. Laughs that made my stomach-ache. Sweet memories shared with friends and family.

But at the end of the day...

There were no hugs. No cuddles. No silly banter during a movie with a glass of wine in hand.

It was just me.

Still, I'm an eternal optimist, even if I sometimes sound like a professional pessimist with a side hustle in sarcasm.

But truthfully? I try to stay focused on the positives.

And I *do* trust the Universe. After all, I've made it this far!

Still breathing, still fighting, still standing—with a roof over my head and food in my belly.

So yeah, I'd say the Universe has delivered. Maybe not *early*, but always *on time*.

As for dating...

Let's just say it's back on hold. Which, honestly, is probably for the best. Not to say I don't occasionally scroll through that one dating app I'm still on, *just in case* that one single *perfect* guy decides to emerge from the shadows of digital limbo. But hey, maybe the Universe has him on a timer, too.

As for timing, I took another break from writing because, truthfully, the past few months had been *brutal*.

Deep in the trenches, hunting for a new place to live—navigating listings, paperwork, showings, and price tags that made me question why I'm not living in a grass hut by the ocean. But after many rejects, I'm proud to say I'm now the *official* owner of a condo. It's a win, in the long run. But getting there?

Grueling. Draining. Expensive. It felt like I should be standing on the street corner with a cardboard sign.

"No work, No Money, Please help."

Nonetheless, it's now ancient history and I'm already lining up trades for renos. Gotta make it my own!

On a brighter note, I'm currently employed with a great company. It's a temporary assignment; however, I believe it's been secured for a few years. The people are solid, the vibe is good, and for the first time in a long time, I feel like I might have found a new home–outside my other new home.

# Chapter 20

As I approached 70, I found myself reflecting on life in a new way. While there were no major revelations, it was clear that I possibly have maybe 10, 20, or at best, 30 years left, and I want to make the most of them. With this realization came a deeper understanding of what truly matters.

For me, it was my children. Every step of the way, I've tried to ensure they were happy and healthy and keep the dysfunction to a minimum. I provided guidance, values, and morals essential in life, encouraging them to be kind and selfless while also loving themselves first.

We do the best we can based on what we know and how we were raised. But as they grow, I've had to let them live their lives, face their struggles, and find my own happiness as well. It's tough when one of them takes a difficult path, but I've learned not to get too caught up in their challenges, because I have my own to navigate as well.

The year had been very difficult, but my optimism for 2025 was still intact. I believed I had put the necessary steps in front of me to make it a more prosperous year. But as a mother, the ultimate goal was to see my children happy and healthy.

It's humbling to realize how finite our lives are, and at times, the lengths we go to in search of happiness and fulfillment can feel almost redundant. Life truly is a fascinating phenomenon. When you consider all the things humans do to navigate it–driven by love, passion, and the basic survival instincts—only to ultimately face death, it really makes you pause and reflect on the bigger picture.

I *am* happily single, but in the depth of my soul, I really do want to have that romantic and passionate love where someone other than my children really care about me and want to take care of me, and vice versa. I think that is a very basic human instinct to connect fully with a partner, physically, spiritually and emotionally. I'm remaining hopeful.

In the end I think it's all about Love. We want to know that we were loved, that we were worthy, and that we made a difference in other people's lives and that we actually mattered.

Perhaps this book is about self-discovery and survival. Being completely honest with yourself and being grateful for the gift you have been given to even exist.

Does it come down to what is my NEXT *struggle?* Or what is my NEXT *adventure*? It's about perception.

# Chapter 21

2025. The calendar changed. It was one day after 2024. Did the Universe care? I'm not sure it even has self-awareness; just an eternal chasm of stardust, atoms and molecules. It has no sense of time. It doesn't know New Year's Eve from a Wednesday. But here on planet Earth, the calendar changed, and with that our mindset resets and we reboot.

So, on December 31 (2024), deciding if I should stay in or find a friend to ring in the New Year, I chose the latter. And off my friend and I went to a new place called the *Tipsy Moose*. (Only in Canada, eh?)

We planned to only have a few drinks and a quick bite, resigning ourselves to the idea that we probably wouldn't even make it to midnight. Our enthusiasm was a bit lackluster. But as the night progressed, and the music and energy reverberated through the restaurant, we quickly became absorbed into the vibe.

We danced, we flirted, despite choking on the pungent body odor of some the guys in our midst. (*And, yes, it was that bad to be notable in my book)*. We were now free spirits.

And speaking of pungent, who should be there but a ghost from my dating past. It seemed the *Thirsty Camel* had run dry and old Teletubby Jacob had exchanged the Camel for the Moose.

He was just metres away in another booth, sitting with, from what I gathered, his date. No judgment, but I feel he leveled down a few notches. My inner bitch aside, he saw me and I saw him, and a bit of awkwardness filled the space between us.

I had to step up, so I wandered over to say a quick hello and Happy New Year. It was short and sweet but long enough for him to regret being such a love-bombing creep. Not that it would have worked out in the long run anyway. Quite frankly, he looked a little rough and it reminded me of the Seinfeld episode where the change in lighting made Jerry's date look either really hot or more like a ghoul. Too funny.

That issue addressed, my attention and flirting became directed towards the DJ, who was busy elevating the party atmosphere with a mixed playlist of dance beats and vibes.

I had noticed him earlier in the evening, *before* I knew he was the DJ, and had already expressed interest to my friend. "He's hot". She laughed. She knew my type. Meanwhile, I'm blowing kisses at him across the room, as one *does*, when wine and tequila hijack your better judgment.

Anyway, reciprocating my interest, the DJ, left his post on several occasions to dance with me, him noting later that it's not something he normally does. I was flattered. And that's when everything went for shit. (You *DO* see a pattern in my narratives, right?!)

I'll admit, I'm not too bad on the dance floor. I've got a few fancy moves tucked in my stilettos, but trying to moonwalk in winter boots?

*Yeah... not my finest idea.*

One step backward and I was rudely reminded of the ever-present force: gravity. Down I went. Fast.

I don't remember the fall, not really. One moment I was upright, mid-groove, the next I was horizontal on the floor. I must've instinctively thrown my arms back to catch myself, but it was all a blur. The DJ rushed over and helped me up, and I brushed myself off with what little dignity I had left. A little sore, sure, but mostly embarrassed (though I didn't let it show).

The night was winding down anyway. Midnight had come and gone – yes, we made it and I'm quite sure I kissed my gal pal on the cheek just to make it official.

As the crowd thinned and the music faded, the DJ and his buddy packed up their gear. Then, without being asked, they walked us out to the car—gentlemen style. (My friend, by the way, was quite okay to drive. I, on the other hand, had generously sampled tequila's seductive charm a few times too many.)

And just as I climbed in, Mr. DJ leaned in and kissed me.

Not a quick peck. Not a drunk smooch. A *real* kiss. The kind that lingers on your lips, in your thoughts—above the tequila fog. The kind that makes you forget about bruised wrists and lumbering footwear.

Side note: I had given him my phone number earlier in the evening upon his request. And he called me (surprisingly) several times over the next two weeks trying to get together with me. One major flaw (okay maybe two). First, he was married, which I found out later, and second, he was only 38. But he didn't seem to care. I did. OMG! Men!

Jumping ahead to the next morning, I woke up with very sore wrists and some major bruising from the palm of my hand halfway up my arm. After several visits to the ER and local clinics for x-rays and bone scans, it was concluded that both my wrists were broken. Yup! That's my life. The medic on-call, who was rather cute (sorry but my radar is always on), smacked on some soul-sucking, freedom-stripping casts that turned me from an independent woman into a helpless T-Rex.

With broken wrists and the loss of the ability to do anything, including wiping my ass, opening a jar or milk carton and combing my hair, my job also went out the window (albeit temporarily – as they promised I could return once I had healed). It was truly life changing, especially living by myself.

To add insult to injury – quite literally – my move to the new condo was only a few weeks away. With both of my wrists still out of commission, I could barely pack a single box or even lift more than two plates at a time. I sat helpless, once again relying on my family to rescue me for yet another move.

My daughter, now a seasoned veteran of my nomadic lifestyle, had perfected the dramatic eye roll and the exasperated sigh every time she heard the words, "I'm moving again." This would be the 20th in my lifetime and she's been roped into at least the last five. Our shared relationship with my wandering ways? Definitely love/hate.

However, just when you think you've got everything under control, along comes Moving Day.

January $25^{th}$. The weather seemed cooperative, the movers were scheduled, my landlord notified and my helpers... you guessed it, my daughter and son-in-law, arrived early and ready to go. That is until they pressed the elevator button to the fifth floor. In absolute horror, we discovered the elevator was not working!

What followed was part two of the nightmare. Luckily (but not really), I bumped into the maintenance guy just as he was entering the lobby. I frantically told him the elevator was down and my moving team had just arrived. My stress, anger and anxiety were off the charts. The maintenance guy? Totally unfazed. He barely blinked but made a call to the elevator people to come out "as soon as possible."

Trying not to make this into a spin-off of my book, here's the short version: the elevator tech showed up about 30 minutes later, but had the wrong key to the mechanical room. Apparently, the locks had recently been changed, and he hadn't been given the new one. And guess who did have it? Mr. cool-as-cucumber maintenance guy, who was already across town on another emergency. Two hours later, a totally different staff member showed up with the correct key.

At this point, my poor movers had already scaled five flights of stairs a hundred times, hauling my furniture down to the truck. The elevator was now irrelevant. My heart bled for them. My knees hurt for them. My back couldn't even fathom it! And much to their credit – they took it in stride. I just felt sick.

The damage was done. It took the movers an extra three hours and cost me an additional $1000.00. I tried to receive some type of compensation from the landlord but they pleaded the "fifth." Not their problem; "these things happen." I'm considering suing but that means a lot of paperwork, forms, time and more frustration, so I've left it pending.

*(With all this suing going on... you'd think/hope I'd meet a single handsome lawyer to sweep me away at some point.)*

Finally settled into my new place, with little T-Rex arms, I lent my car to my middle grandson to drive to school, after some sincere begging on his part – since I was unable to drive. But he was ecstatic (and also genuinely grateful). My family pitched in whenever they could, but at the end of the day, I had to reinvent how I cooked, ate, showered, slept, and all things relating to personal care and mental health. I was like a 2-year-old toddler trying to figure out how to hold a cup and spoon again.

It was a long 9 ½ weeks of recovery. When the casts/splints finally came off, I felt like the butterfly emerging from the restraints of the cocoon. I had forgotten what happiness felt like. But once again I was happy!

As the weeks passed, I took a new lease on life, with much gratitude, and felt ready to start the New Year properly. And it was now March! My 70th birthday was coming up. I had much to celebrate.

I organized a wonderful celebration with all my closest friends at a local restaurant/pub, in their private dining room. Great stories, trivia games (like 20 Questions About "Me" to test if they were even listening to me over the years) and good old drinking set the tone for the whole night.

The energy was high and I looked and felt great! The fact that I was in my 7th decade didn't even phase me. In my mind, I was still 50-something.

With strength, dignity, kindness, integrity and a sense of humour in my *old kit bag,* I had kept afloat through every disastrous day or year I had ever endured. And there were plenty. But as the ying and yang of life presents itself, I also had some of the best moments anyone could ever imagine.

# Chapter 22

At this point in my story, I was considering wrapping it up with some awe-inspiring quotes and nuggets of wisdom, but, alas, another opponent entered the ring just before curtain call.

*Ding, ding ding!* Round 20 chimed in the eternal arena of dating and I blindly remained hopeful that *this* could be the One. Pathetic, I know, but without hope, you might as well dig a deep hole, jump in and throw dirt on your face.

As I entered the arena once again, bouncing off the side ropes in hopes of cushioning my fall on a firm but soft body, the NEXT contender arrived. Let's call him Mike Tyson (if only to keep the boxing reference going). Easy on the eyes, a firm body and checking most of my must-have boxes. We slowly, and mostly last minute, (insert red flag) set up dates, swapped life stories and aligned our energies.

The downside (cuz, there always is *one*) was his crazy bus driver shifts and commitments around them. When not behind the big wheel, he was either a gym rat pumping up his biceps or zoning out on his guitar (his words), so there wasn't much left for playtime. At least with me.

During the whole month I knew him, we had a total of three dates, in between fun text messages that were respectful and sweet. I was taking it slow, completely against my usual pattern of meet/greet/sleep (with). I had progressed, and was no longer willing to give it up before I knew *they* were worthy.

But on one lovely day in April, after some surprisingly intimate and revealing banter, with him concluding "I can't wait to see you", it all went *dead.* No cutesy texts, no "Good morning, Sexy." It just ended.

In one last ditch effort–more floating out a tester–I sent a quick text two days later, noting my court trial date was that morning and I was feeling a bit nervous. He replied with a, "you got this, head up, shoulders back!"

But as I waited for even a feigned morsel of a follow-up later that day (i.e.: "How'd it go?"), it never arrived. I surmised he was gone. Ghosted once again!

Disappointed, I figuratively tossed him out in the back shed with all the other rotting skeletons of rejects, repeating my quick farewell mantra, "Fuck you!"

And this is where the *mystery* lies. (insert foreshadowing here).

Did he get scared? Did he get the *feels*? Or feared losing his guy time? We will never really know. Or... is this only on a *back burner.* Stay tuned.

Coincidentally, on the same day, I stumbled across a blog or profile (as if planted by the *dating angels*) on Facebook from a guy who seemed to be writing the male version of my book! Although he uses F-bombs way more liberally than I, he had some bold (and cold) insights! Simple, straight to the point and no fluff. No mystery.

I responded to one of his posts asking if I could quote him in my book (giving him creds, of course) and he was more than "f...king" happy to oblige.

His response... and I quote:

*"That sounds fucking fantastic! Love that you're bringing humour and raw truth to the dating chaos from the female perspective – we need more of that. And fuck yeah, feel free to quote whatever resonates..."*

So, allow me to invite and indulge you in his perspective (now part of *my* book) to throw some high beams on men.

Author: *"Zen Prem"*

*He's just not that into you – and you Fucking know it!*

*Alright, let's cut the shit. You already know the answer, but here you are – scouring his texts like they're some lost Dead Sea Scroll that'll reveal his true feelings. One kiss emoji? Just an "x"? Holy shit – why didn't he go full "xxx"?! What does it mean?!*

*It means nothing. Because if a man wants you, you won't be sitting here playing forensic linguist with his half-arsed messages. You'll know. And if you're still breaking down punctuation, timing, and emoji patterns like you're cracking an unsolved crime, here's the truth:*

*He's not into you. And you fucking know it.*

*Because I'm a man. And men aren't that complicated.*

*And yet, here you fucking are – still analysing emojis like they're ancient scrolls from the Oracle of Mixed Signals.*

*If a man wants you, you won't be refreshing WhatsApp at 1:12a.m., replaying his last "haha" wondering if it felt colder than usual.*

*How many times have you made excuses for a man who treats you like an optional extra?*

*"He's just bad at texting"*

*No, he's just bad at caring.*

*"He's scared of commitment."*

*No, he's just not scared of losing you.*

*"He likes to take things slow"*

*No, he likes keeping you on standby while he explores his options.*

*As I say, Men aren't complicated. When we want something, we go after it. If he's not calling, not texting, not showing up, that's not a* ***mystery****. That's your answer."*

So, there you go! Mystery solved! He did write a bit more, but I think you get the (harsh) gist of it.

Personally, I feel it provided the figurative face slap that we need to stop clouding our dating minds and overthinking every comma, emoji and how many "x's" he used. It's all too true. And I say Thank you! Click Follow.

NOW, let's spin back to my court day! At least this brought some much-needed positive energy.

After eleven months of claims served, affidavits sworn and notarized, and several trips to the Court House to file said documents, we came to the conclusion.

The night before, with nervous energy buzzing through me, I was worried I might not sleep. The brain spun. But, nonetheless, I managed to fall into a jangled and sporadic slumber. I had about six or seven hours of dreaming I was in court. Random clips that didn't make a whole lot of sense but such is the subconscious mind. Nonetheless, alarm set for 6:30am, I got through my morning routine and headed off.

I was greeted by my legal agent in suit, tie, sharp and professional specs that added a distinguished flair to his 23 years, and exuding a smile of confidence. He was accompanied by a school mate to observe the hearing.

Of course, me being me, I felt compelled to share my night of crazy dreams of being in court all night long. They both chimed in in unison, "Perfectly natural." We all laughed.

So not to bore you with all the usual courtroom drama, let's just say that my agent, Trevor, was on fire! This was only his second time in court, and from what little I know about legal theatrics, he nailed it. A regular Perry Mason. Okay, maybe I've just dated myself back to the Stone Age, but you get the idea. Even the judge gave high praise at the end.

Trevor had an entire binder, complete with colored tabs, full of meticulous behind the scenes research. As he laid out the messy details of my situation, citing case law like a pro, with several back up references to similar cases and their outcomes, I was majorly impressed.... And mildly turned on. Not in a sexual way, but the type that comes from watching power and confidence combine. Who knew this young man, with impish charm and adorable nerdiness, could present himself so well?

After the judge reviewed all that was presented, including my personal testimony of strife and hardship, while trembling in the daunting witness booth, he dropped (figuratively) the gavel. Judgment was made and I was awarded a good chunk of what we were claiming. It was fair and just and I was happy.

Court adjourned and out in the common area, away from the microphones and cameras, Trevor and I collapsed into a mammoth hug, him squeezing me much harder and longer than I was anticipating. There was relief in that hug. We could all breathe again.

As my lengthy journey through the legal arena unfolded, I eventually hired a licensed lawyer to take the reins. The necessary steps were completed, the money was received, and just like that—case closed!

Exhale.

So, is this the end? Not even close! Such words should never be uttered! Knowing me and how much life I still have to live, I've still got a lot of mountains to climb and unknowns to conquer. But I will say this....

The guy on the *back burner* (aka: Mike Tyson) came back a few days later and he hasn't missed a day since. Consistent, listening to my needs, accepting my boundaries, and a little obsessed with me, dates are adding up, intimate moments have been *notched* and differences acknowledged, or at least accepted. Could he be the ONE? Or *NEXT*?

## IN CLOSING

On the bright side and in my quest to find the somewhat perfect guy for me, I have learned quite a bit about myself. Aside from dating sites being a total waste of time (as 90% are fake profiles or guys just killing time with no intent to meet), I have learned that I won't settle for mediocrity; that I won't change who I am (or adjust) for any guy. This doesn't mean not compromising; it means if he can't handle the real me, my past stories and what I need to thrive, then he's not the one. It's also allowed me to see clearly through all the bullshit that men (and I suppose women) put out there. Reading profiles and honing my skills for catching red flags and undesirable personality traits, has given me tremendous insight into what to avoid at all costs. And for this, I can be grateful.

And perhaps this could and should be my closing paragraph in reference to the very beginning of this story. I now realize that Keith was totally not the right guy for me. Aside from laughing a lot, and the fact we were very sexually compatible, he didn't make the cut. He was kind of like a little old woman (in Pickleball gear), worrying and fretting about things that weren't worth fretting about, and the fact that anyone younger than 60 was too young for him (he was 68). "We'll have nothing in common to talk about," was his go to concern. For me, age was never a factor for making new friends and connections. To sum it up... he had an avoidant attachment style and too many traumas hiding in the cobwebs of his mind.

In the end... of *this* story ...my journey has given me the knowledge and experience to know what I want and need going into my next relationship.

Will I find it?

***ABOUT THE AUTHOR:***

*Sharon has been writing short stories since her high school days. When she should have been completing assignments from the typing textbook, she was instead crafting imaginative tales filled with fantastical characters. That creative spark eventually evolved into humorous editorials, newsletters, and storytelling later in her adult life and professional career.*

*This short memoir is a reflection of her chaotic, quirky, and wonderfully unique life—told through a lighthearted and hopeful lens. No matter what life throws her way, she believes in finding the irony, the beauty, and the will to survive.*

*Sharon brings her signature blend of raw truth, humor, and heart to this latest work. Think: diary meets stand-up comedy meets deeply human memoir.*

www.ingramcontent.com/pod-product-compliance
Lightning Source LLC
Chambersburg PA
CBHW030941111125
35264CB00020B/128
* 9 7 9 8 2 3 2 5 3 4 6 1 5 *